Folk Dance
Handbook

by Marcia Eastman Snider

HANCOCK HOUSE PUBLISHERS

ISBN 0-88839-044-0 pa.

Copyright © 1980 Snider, Marcia Eastman

These books have been prepared for the Ministry of
Education, Province of British Columbia, under the
direction of the Secondary Physical Education
Curriculum Revision Committee (1980)

James Appleby   John Lowther
Alex Carre   Mike McKee
Madeline Gemmill   Norman Olenick
Gerry Gilmore   David Turkington
George Longstaff

Handbook Consultant: F. Alex Carre, Ph.D.

Canadian Cataloguing in Publication Data

Snider, Marcia Eastman.
    Folk dancing and curriculum guide
(Physical education series)

    Bibliography: p.
    ISBN 0-88839-044-0 pa.
    1. Folk dancing - Study and teaching. I. Title.
II. Series: Physical Education Series (North
Vancouver, B.C.)
GV1753.5.S64   793.3'1'0712   C80-091139-3

Editor Margaret Campbell
Design Paul Willies & Donna White
Production Tom Morgan
Typeset by Donna White & Dana Cleland *in Megaron type on an AM Varityper Comp/Edit*

Printed in Canada

Published by
HANCOCK HOUSE PUBLISHERS LTD.
#10 Orwell St., North Vancouver, B.C. Canada V7J 3K1

Table of Contents

Chapter Four

Sample Lesson Plans

Chapter Five

Evaluation

Chapter Six
Dance Descriptions

Acknowledgments

I would like to acknowledge and thank Dick Crum, Michael and Mary Ann Herman, Dale Hyde, Gordon Tracie, Marlys Waller, Jane Harris and Anne Pittman for granting permission to use their dance descriptions. Special thanks should go to Richard Spratley, Sarah, Rohan, Terry and Geoffrey for their research and photographic assistance.

Chapter One
Introduction

A. Introduction: What is Folk Dance?

The term *folk dance* has several connotations. In its broadest sense, it refers to a form of dance done by ordinary people (rather than by professionals or specialists), primarily for their *own* recreational enjoyment, to meet a variety of personal and social needs. These needs may involve courtship, reinforcement of a sense of community, emotional expression and release of physical tension, and worship or celebration of important events in life. In pre-industrial peasant societies, both exercise and physical effort were natural components of daily life. However, in modern urban societies, folk dance meets the need for an enjoyable leisure-time activity which increases the level of physical fitness.

A narrower definition of *folk dance* (or, as it is sometimes called, *international* folk dance) would restrict its meaning to the traditional dance cultures of "foreign" nations or ethnic areas. Used in this sense, it is seen as separate from the North American heritage of dance forms such as Western square dance, New England contra dance, and dances from Appalachia and French Canada as well as universally popular forms of "social" dance such as ballroom, disco, and so forth, which cross ethnic boundaries. A rigorous definition which emphasizes the traditional aspect, would also exclude choreographed adaptations using ethnic steps and styling.

Looking at the repertory of many North American recreational folk dance groups, one can see both definitions in operation. On the one hand, some groups tend to specialize in one or more related types of ethnic dance (Israeli, Balkan, or Scandinavian, for example) and to work more intensively on traditional styling. Other groups are gradually increasing the types of dance in their repertory to include the occasional Western square, Appalachian, or French Canadian dance, as well as novelty dances and perhaps even a bit of jive or disco.

Ultimately, the choice of definition is one which each individual teacher must make, taking into consideration the needs and interests of the students or group members. Because the material in this handbook is oriented primarily toward the secondary Physical Education student, it uses a fairly broad definition of folk dance, including in the selection of dances a French Canadian dance as representative of one aspect of the Canadian dance heritage, as well as several currently popular novelty-type dances which are an enjoyable way to learn some of the traditional step patterns. However, it is extremely important to distinguish between choreographed arrangements and traditional dances which have evolved over the years as a meaningful expression of a people's ethnic individuality. While dance may be a peripheral and casual part of our modern North American culture, it plays, or has played a central and deeply important role in many other cultures. One should respect and help preserve the integrity of each ethnic tradition by teaching and performing both the sequences and the styling of the dances as accurately as possible.

B. Purpose of the Handbook

This handbook is designed for use by secondary school Physical Education instructors as an extension of the basic philosophy and program presented in the 1980 Secondary Physical Education Curriculum and Resource Guide. However, it is hoped that the information will be helpful to elementary school teachers and recreational folk dance leaders as well.

C. Handbook Format

The handbook presents a developmental progression of folk dance skills and knowledge keyed to the folk dance Activity Sequence Chart. Sample lesson plans built around a suggested selection of folk dances are included, as well as information necessary for the application of this material to the classroom situation. Because of space limitations, emphasis is on the introductory and beginning material in Levels I and II, but there is also some discussion of the turning skills explored in Level III.

The progressions and dances outlined are only suggested ones. There are other possible progression sequences and a vast number of folk dances from which to choose. The number of dances which could be included in this handbook is necessarily small. The Bibliography contains other more ample collections of dance descriptions. The particular dances described in this handbook were selected on the basis that: a) they are dances which are popular, not only with secondary students but in recreational folk dance clubs as well, b) they are dances which are adaptable to different numbers and types of groups, and c) they are dances for which records are readily available, at least at the present time.

D. Objectives of the Program

Looking at long range objectives, the initial experience of folk dance within the Physical Education curriculum can lead to successful participation in folk dance as a lifelong recreational activity. This type of recreational activity can not only maintain and improve physical fitness, but also, since it is group-oriented, help to increase social skills and enjoyment as well. In addition, the students' experience of varied forms of cultural expression through dance will hopefully increase their tolerance and understanding of different racial and ethnic groups.

In the more immediate sense, a secondary school program of folk dance should aim to achieve three major objectives:

1. Psychomotor Objectives

a) Students' increased ability to perceive and control their own bodies in motion.
b) Mastery of the fundamental forms of locomotion.
c) Mastery of a graded series of traditional step patterns.
d) Mastery of a graded series of dance sequences in which the above are incorporated.
e) An increase in the ability to coordinate the movements of the entire body so as to produce the appropriate quantity and timing of dynamic effort.
f) An increase in rhythmic skill; the ability to time movements so that they correlate with the music.
g) An increase in spatial skills; the ability to control the size, direction and level of each movement so as to complete the required spatial designs in a given amount of time.
h) An increased level of physical fitness and agility.

2. Cognitive Objectives

a) The students' understanding of the basic principles of human motion can be increased.
b) The students' understanding of rhythmic analysis and comprehension of specific dance terminology can be increased.
c) The dances can be viewed in the context of their cultural background and can be correlated with associated areas of cognitive experience such as social studies, history, language, music, and others.

3. Affective Objectives

a) Development of the ability to act cooperatively and with courtesy and consideration for others.
b) Increased skill in leading and following.
c) Development of confidence in his or her own movement skill and ability to meet the increased challenges offered by succeeding levels in this activity.
d) To experience dance as a source of enjoyment and a positive physical/psychological release activity.
e) To feel at ease dancing with members of the opposite sex.

E. Application to Classroom Instruction

Classroom instruction of folk dance will be aided by a consideration of the learning environment, elements involved in planning a developmental series of lessons, and effective teaching strategies.

1. Environment

The appropriate learning environment is extremely important. Such factors as the available space, sound equipment, clothing and supplemental teaching aids must be considered.

a) Physical features
The most crucial factor is a large, open room, if possible with a resilient wood or linoleum-covered wood floor, rather than concrete which, if used for vigorous running and jumping dances, can cause foot and leg injuries. Either too slippery a surface or a rough or carpeted surface can make traveling types of movement awkward and hazardous. Adjustable heating controls or windows which can be opened will add to the comfort and enjoyment of the session.

b) Sound system
An adequate sound system should consist of a variable-speed record player (so that steps and dances can be practiced slowly at first, then at gradually increased speeds until up to tempo); a microphone, if the room is large; and speakers which are sufficiently powerful and placed so that the sound can be heard clearly everywhere in the room. Check this carefully before beginning. In many gyms, reverberation may make it difficult to hear the basic underlying beat of the music. Another valuable aid is a cassette tape recorder. Most lack the ability to slow down or speed up the music but several tapings of the same piece at different speeds may solve this problem. If a number of small, portable cassette recorders and tapes can be made available for student use outside of class time or in class, so that several groups can work separately in different corners of the room, it will encourage individual initiative and greater achievement, and *facilitate multi-level teaching*. An organized and protective filing system for records and cassettes will increase accessibility and help preserve sound quality.

c) Teaching aids
Additional teaching aids such as a blackboard, a bulletin board for maps and pictures, films and video tapes will augment and enrich the program.

d) Clothing
Students should wear comfortable clothing for strenuous activity and runners or low-heeled, flexible shoes or slippers. More advanced dancers will find that a belt, a kerchief, or a skirt may be needed for particular

dances. For informal performances, a set of sashes and boleros can turn shirts and pants or skirts into inexpensive but attractive costumes. However, if interest and expenses permit, researching and making a simple ethnic costume can enrich the folk dance experience.

2. Planning lessons

In *planning* a series of folk dance lessons, the instructor should:

a) Select dances which are suited to the interest and ability of the students.
b) Include a number of non-partner line and circle dances, individual dances and trios to ease self-consciousness about partner relationships, and mixers to allow students to meet each other. When working on partner steps and dances, have students change partners a number of times. However, provide enough time between these changes to allow the development of a feeling of teamwork.
c) Select a varied and balanced group of dances in terms of tempo, energy level, formation and country or ethnic area of origin.
d) Know each dance and its music thoroughly.

F. Description of Levels Approach

The folk dance skills and activities presented in this handbook have been organized into a developmental sequence of four stages or levels of difficulty which provide a framework for individual progress and growth in psychomotor, cognitive and affective learning areas.

In folk dance at the present time, there is no generally accepted standardized instruction program or list of levels guidelines such as exists in tennis, for example. The progression described in this handbook is one which is accepted and used by many instructors.

The four-level system used in this handbook is as follows:

Level I	- Beginner
Level II	- Novice
Level III	- Intermediate
Level IV	- Advanced

Level I is designed as a review or an introduction to those fundamental rhythmic and locomotor skills needed for successful and enjoyable folk dance experiences. In particular, it emphasizes understanding and mastery of the basic forms of locomotion (walking, running, hopping, jumping, and so on) and a variety of simple dances in which they can be practiced.

Level II focuses on some widely-known traditional *combinations* of these basic locomotor steps such as the schottische, polka, and so on, in their most simple form and introduces rhythmic and spatial patterning. The development of a "vocabulary" of frequently-used step patterns will aid future learning.

Level III increases the skill challenge by presenting

previously learned traditional step patterns in more difficult forms (such as turning), adding additional step patterns to the students' vocabulary, and presenting dance sequences which are structurally more complex.

The content of Level IV must depend not only on the interests of the students but also on the experience and background of the instructor. There is a diversity of dance material from which to choose and the instructor or students may want to specialize in one or several related ethnic areas, or to polish, perfect and costume a few more complex dances for demonstrations or performances. Accuracy of styling should be emphasized and the instructor and students would be advised to attend clubs, workshops by ethnic specialists, or to draw on ethnic resources within the community if possible.

G. Explanation of the Activity Sequence Chart

The following Activity Sequence Chart lists a skill progression starting with fundamental movement principles, then presenting a sequence of skills in a) fundamental locomotor skills, and b) traditional locomotor step patterns or combinations of the basic forms of locomotion. It also lists associated formation, handhold, position and directional terminology with which the student should become familiar. It includes lists of dance choices (in order of difficulty from simple to complex) which make predominant use of each particular fundamental locomotor coordination or traditional locomotor step pattern.

A number of options are given for each step so that the instructor can choose the dance or dances which suit the needs and interests of his or her own group.

Note: *Multi-level* teaching within one class may be necessary to meet the need of individual students to progress at their own rate.

H. Activity Sequence Chart

SKILLS	I	II	III	IV
A. Fundamental Principles				
1. Control of balance in axial movement and weight transference (locomotion)	●			
2. Development of rhythmic ability: moving with the musical beat and in simple rhythmic patterns	●			
B. Fundamental Locomotor Skills				
1. Walk	●			
2. Run	●			
3. Hop (from one foot onto same foot)	●			
4. Jump (from one or both feet onto both feet)	●			
5. Leap (from one foot onto the other foot)	●			
6. Gallop (run with uneven rhythm)	●			
7. Slide (side gallop)	●			
8. Step-hop (even rhythm)	●			
9. Skip (step-hop with uneven rhythm)	●			
10. Stamp				
a) taking weight	●			
b) not taking weight	●			
C. Traditional Locomotor Step Patterns				
1. Touch-step	●			
2. Schottische				
a) forward		●		
b) with step-hop couple turn			●	
c) with spatial variations			●	
3. Two-step				
a) forward		●		
b) couple, turning			●	
4. Polka				
a) forward		●		
b) heel-toe Polka		●		
c) couple turning			●	
5. Skip change of step		●		
6. Mazurka		●		
7. Waltz				
a) forward		●		
b) couple, turning			●	
8. Bleking jump	●			

SKILLS	I	II	III	IV
9. Grapevine step and other crossing steps		●		
10. Hora-Hassapikos step		●		
11. Couple turn, walking	●			
12. Couple turn, Buzz-step			●	
13. Pas de Basque		●		
14. Hungarian break step "Bokazo"	●			
15. Yemenite step			●	
16. Debka jump			●	
17. Syrtos			●	
18. Hop-step-step			●	
19. Lesnoto, basic			●	
20. 'Basic' kolo step				●
21. 'Syncopated' threes				●
22. Skoci step				●
23. Pivot turn				●
24. Hambo step				●
25. Pols				●
26. Hopsa step			●	
27. Prysyadkas				●
D. Basic Dance Formations				
1. No partners:				
a) circle: facing center, clockwise, or counterclockwise	●			
b) line or open circle	●			
c) scatter formation	●			
2. Partner:				
a) single circle: partners facing	●			
b) double circle: men with backs to center, facing partners	●			
c) double circle: partners side by side facing counter-clockwise	●			
d) longways or contra formation				
- line of men facing line of women	●			
- partners side by side: facing up or down set	●			
- lines alternating men and women: partners facing	●			
e) couple scatter	●			

H. Activity Sequence Chart

SKILLS	I	II	III	IV
f) double circle, couples facing: 'Sicilian Circle'	●			
g) Trios, 'Wheelspoke' formation, all facing counter-clockwise	●			
h) trios in 'Sicilian Circle' formation	●			
E. Basic Dance Handholds and Positions				
1. Line or Circle:				
a) 'V' or arms straight down	●			
b) 'W' handhold elbows bent	●			
c) 'T' or shoulder hold		●		
d) front basket hold		●		
e) back basket hold			●	
f) little finger hold		●		
2. Couple				
a) social dance or waltz hold	●			
b) inside hand hold	●			
c) 2-hand hold or ring grasp	●			
d) elbow hook	●			
e) shoulder-waist position		●		
f) Varsouvienne position		●		
g) swing position		●		
h) western promenade or skater's hold	●			
i) conversation position	●			
F. Basic Folk Dance Directions				
1. Circle left: clockwise	●			
2. Circle right: counterclockwise	●			
3. Line of Dance: (LOD), counterclockwise	●			
4. Reverse line of dance: (RLOD), clockwise	●			
5. "Snaking" the line	●			
6. Spiraling the line	●			
G. Dances Using Fundamental Locomotor Coordinations * †				
1. Walk:				
Ve David	●			
Fjäskern	●			
Pljeskavac	●			
Pljeskavac w/step-hops		●		
Apat Apat		●		
Tino Mori			●	
2. Run:				
Troika	●			
Knodeldrahner		●		
Kentucky Running Set		●		

SKILLS	I	II	III	IV
3. Step-Hop				
Crested Hen	●			
Šetnja		●		
4. Skip:				
D'Hammerschmiedsgselln	●			
Man in the Hay		●		
Windmueller			●	
5. Jump:				
La Raspa	●			
Bleking	●			
Hora Aggadati			●	
Haro'a Haktana				●
6. Slide:				
Cumberland Reel	●			
Virginia Reel	●			
Gigue aux Six	●			
Gigue aux Six w/gigue steps		●		
7. Stamp:				
Alunelul		●		
Tropanka (Hermans)		●		
Tropanka from Dobrudja			●	
H. Dances Using Traditional Locomotor Step Patterns † *				
1. Touch-Step				
Alley Cat	●			
Pata Pata	●			
Amos Moses		●		
2. Schottische:				
a) (forward/backward)				
Ersko Kolo		●		
Savila se bela Loza		●		
Korobushka		●		
b) (dance pattern):				
Horse and Buggy Schottische		●		
Salty Dog Rag		●		
c) (with couple turn):				
freestyle with variations			●	
Marklaender Schottische				●
3. Two-step:				
a) forward: Cotton-Eyed Joe				
Kicker Dance		●		
Oklahoma Trio Mixer		●		
b) turning: Boston Two-Step			●	
The Gay Gordons			●	
"with Pas de Basque"				●
Karapyet				●
4. Polka:				
a) forward: Klumpakojis		●		

SKILLS	I	II	III	IV
b) heel-toe: Polka zu Dreien		•		
c) couple turn: Doudlebska Polka			•	
Zigeuner Polka			•	
d) with lift: Kanafaska				•
5. Waltz:				
a) forward: Norwegian Mountain March		•		
Spinnradl		•		
b) turning:Tyrolean Waltz			•	
Little Man in a Fix			•	
Zillertaler Laendler				•
6. Mazurka:				
Israeli Mazurka		•		
Swedish Varsouvienne			•	
Kreuz Koenig				•
7. Grapevine Step and other Crossing Steps:				
Seljančica		•		
Simi Yadech		•		
Armenian Misirlou		•		
Mayim			•	
Harmonica			•	
Vulpiţa				•
8. Yemenite Step:				
Ma Na'avu			•	
At Va'ani			•	
9. Debka Jump:				
Mechol Ovadya			•	
with variations 3 and 4				•
Debka, Debka				•
10. Skip Change of Step and Pas de Basque:				
Dashing White Sergeant			•	
Duke of Perth				•
11. Hop-Step-Step:				
Seljančica Kolo			•	
Sukačko			•	
Godečki Čačak				•
12. Hopsa (and waltz):				
Svensk Maskerade				•
13. 'Basic' Kolo Step:				
Seljancič̌a Kolo (advanced version)				•
U Šest				•
14. 'Syncopated' Threes and Skoči Step:				
U Šest				•

SKILLS	I	II	III	IV
15. Pivot Turn:				
To Ting				•
Norwegian Polka				•
Vossarul				•

*Dances listed in order of difficulty
†Each skill has several optional/alternative dance selections listed.
Not all dances are required.

I. Relationship of Folk Dance to Goals and Learning Outcomes

A series of Goals and Learning Outcomes for physical education were developed for the Secondary Physical Education Curriculum and Resource Guide (1980). The relationship of folk dance to the four major goals of this Curriculum Guide is indicated in the following paragraph.

One of the aims of the secondary school folk dance program should be to encourage students to continue participation in later years. Folk dance as a lifelong recreational activity can improve physical fitness and coordination through achievement of psychomotor goals, increase knowledge of different cultures, and provide many social benefits as well.

Chapter Two
Teaching Strategies and Dance Terminology

A. General Teaching Strategies

Skill development in folk dance is achieved through the practice of a graded series of specific motor and rhythmic skills presented in the context of a variety of folk dances. It also involves the acquisition of knowledge and skill in joining together with a partner or a group in various positions, handholds and formations to travel on various types of paths moving in different directions.

In the following outline of folk dance skills and teaching techniques, a notation system is used to diagram and clarify the essential elements of each skill. Specific terms for various handholds, positions, formations and directions are used as well.

The following strategies should improve *teaching effectiveness*.

1. Instruction should be fast-paced and progressive to improve motivation and interest, and allow as much active movement as possible. Many students learn movement skills more quickly if the explanation is accompanied by a visual demonstration.

2. Be consistent in the use of standard terminology when organizing the group into formations and positions, describing basic steps and traditional step patterns, and explaining the directional elements of the sequence.

3. Allow time for student input, initiative and creativity.

4. Encourage students to listen to the music, feel the basic underlying beat, be aware of the melodic phrasing and coordinate the timing of their movements to fit the music.

5. When teaching a complex dance sequence, use verbal cues slightly ahead of the phrasing of the music to remind students of the sequence while they are still struggling with the individual steps. However, as soon as possible, give them the responsibility for remembering the sequence without visual or verbal reliance on the instructor.

6. Most importantly, enjoy folk dancing yourself and be confident of your own abilities and your students' enjoyment and success.

7. Enrich the learning experience by using brief presentations describing the background of the dance, visual aids and resources available from students, parents and local ethnic groups. Wherever possible, work with instructors in other related subjects such as history and geography.

B. Teaching Strategies for Multi-level Classes

1. Teach the basic locomotor step or traditional step pattern to the whole class then, in smaller groups, divided by skill level, teach, have an assistant teach, or have the students themselves work out from the dance description, the particular dance sequence using that step which is best suited to their level.

   Note: If students are working out a dance description, it is essential that they have a clear understanding of the principles of rhythmic analysis and the dance terminology used.

2. Many folk dances, particularly Greek and Balkan line and circle dances, have a simple basic pattern followed optionally by a more challenging version or by several variations often done at the leader's discretion. In the original village setting, the simple version was designed so that everyone, including often the very young and the elders of the community could participate, and it is often possible and ethnically permissible to have different people in the line or circle doing different variations simultaneously. In a multi-level class, groups of more skillful and advanced students could work on variations and/or could take turns leading lines and calling their own sequence of variations, while beginning students continue to work on mastery of the basic pattern.

3. In couple dances, a traditional step pattern plus a number of figure variations may be done free-style, led by the man. Again the basic step pattern can be mastered by all, then the additional variations practiced, each couple working at their own level.

4. Even in some more formal set dances, dancers may add optional embellishments. In New England contra dances a varied repertory of balance steps is admired. In many French Canadian dances, gigue steps may be done by inactive dancers dancing in place. In Appalachian Big Circle dancing, different clogging steps are a recent addition, adding variety and creativity.

   In most ethnic dance traditions, there is considerable

leeway and encouragement of individual embellishment, enrichment, or innovation within the inherited dance structure. Each culture reserves the right to prescribe the specific areas and ways in which this is permissible. If one allows total creative freedom in changing a traditional dance, perhaps adding movements or styling from other cultures, either deliberately or accidentally, one is contributing to the destruction of each culture's individuality of expression — a beautiful but fragile heritage!

Note: Wherever possible, in the dance lists and particularly in the sample lesson plans included in this handbook, dances have been selected *which lend themselves to multi-level teaching.* Hopefully, however, the pursuit of personal skill achievement goals will not be allowed to detract from the social values and enjoyment to be gained from participation in folk dance as a cooperative group activity. Simple, familiar dances can be enjoyed by people of all levels of ability and experience as long as opportunities for challenge are built into the program as well.

LIST OF ABBREVIATIONS

M	man or men	RLOD	reverse line of dance (CW)
W	woman, women	RH	right hand
Ptr., ptrs.	partner or partners	LH	left hand
cpl., cpls.	couple, couples	ft.	foot or feet
R	right	ftwk.	footwork
L	left	opp.	opposite
fwd.	forward	opp. ftwk.	opposite footwork
twd.	toward	wt.	weight
ctr.	center	meas.	measure or bar of music
bk.	back	ct., cts.	count, counts
diag.	diagonal or diagonally	S	slow
CW	clockwise	Q	quick
CCW	counter-clockwise	Fig.	dance figure
LOD	line of dance (CCW)	tog.	together

C. Rhythm and Movement Notation System

This basic form of notation has been used previously by Margaret H'Doubler and other dance authors. It is useful primarily for notating rhythmic patterns and locomotor movement sequences. It has the virtues of simplicity and ease of reading and writing since it does not require a knowledge of musical notation. It is not intended for use as a comprehensive notation of total body movement.

a) Basic Underlying Beat

— — — — — —

1. Dashes indicate the *Basic Underlying Beat* or Pulse. Note that this is even, regular and unpatterned.
2. The speed or tempo of this series of beats is not indicated in this system.

b) Beat Groupings

2/ |— —|— —|——|

4/ |— — — —|— —:— —|

1. Vertical bar lines indicate *grouping* of this beat into measures as in musical notation.
2. Measures may be in groups of 2, 3, 4, 6, 7, 9, and so on.
3. In cases where the traditional locomotor step pattern starts or ends at a point *within* the measure, a dotted vertical bar line indicates this.

c) Divided Beats

one   and

one   and   'a'

one   'a'   and   'a'

1. The basic beat can be *divided* into beats which are 2, 3, or 4 times as fast as indicated by small dashes *above* the Basic Underlying Beat line.
2. One common way of counting them verbally is written above.

d) Combined Beats

1. The basic beat can be *combined* into beats which are 2, 3, or 4 times as slow, as indicated by long dashes above the basic beat line.

e) Rhythmic Combinations

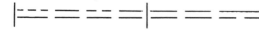

1. A rhythmic *pattern* is a varied combination of some or all of the above rhythmic elements as in the sample given.

Note: Additional movement information can be listed above or below the Basic Underlying Beat and Rhythmic Pattern. In this handbook, the skill diagrams will also describe the following movement aspects, if pertinent.

f) Dynamics   ◢ strong accent

◢ lighter or secondary accent

1. Lists both the general level of energy expediture or degree of forcefulness, and those points within the movement pattern which have an increase in energy expenditure. Indicated by accent marks.

g) Step

1. In this system the locomotor step is listed normally above the beat on which the movement lands; the time at which the transfer of weight is *completed*.
2. For a definition of each basic locomotor step see the discussion of fundamental locomotor skills in chapter three.

| h) Weight Transference: | R = Right
L = Left
L̲R̲ = Weight on both feet | 1. Awareness of weight transfer and which foot is supporting the body weight may not be important in simple dances using unpatterned walking or running steps. However, in more complex locomotor patterns, and in dances with changes of direction, it is often crucial.
2. This type of movement awareness is not well developed in many people and may require constant reinforcement. |

i) Spatial Factors

1. Describes various changes of position in space--direction, change of level, movement size, position of leg or foot relative to the other leg or the rest of the body, and so on.

j) Styling

1. Refers to ways of shaping a step pattern which are specific to a particular ethnic culture, as well as general factors involving good use of body mechanics to produce ease and grace of movement.

D. Dance Directions

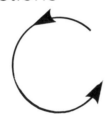

= CCW (counterclockwise, anticlockwise)
LOD (Line of Dance Direction)

= CW (clockwise)
RLOD (Reverse Line of Dance Direction)

= 'Snaking' the Line

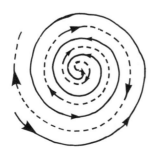

= 'Spiraling' the line in
(One may also double back at the center, reversing the circular direction to spiral out)

E. Dance Formations

Key

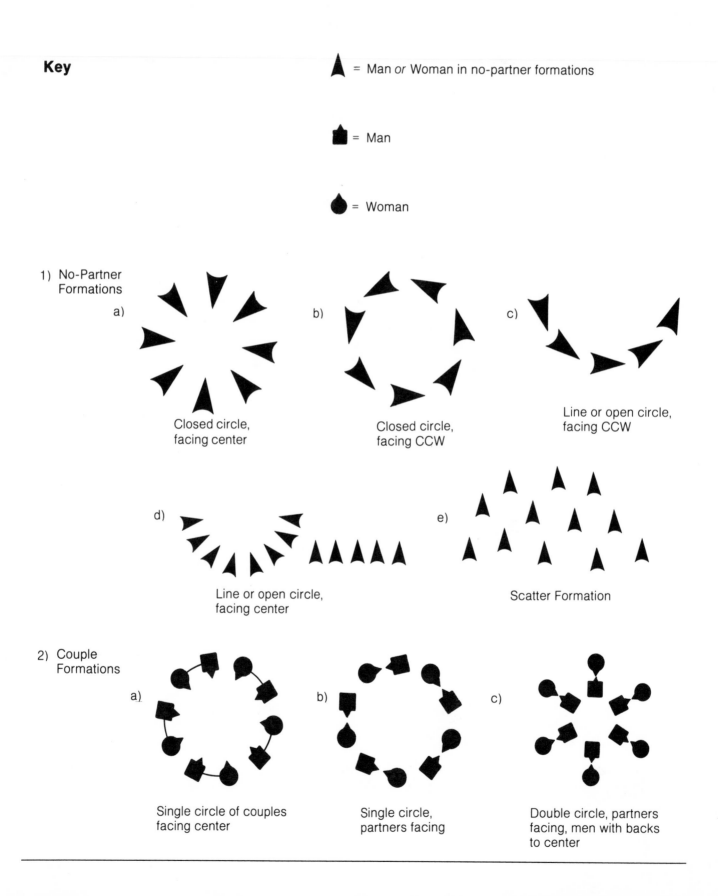

= Man *or* Woman in no-partner formations

= Man

= Woman

1) No-Partner Formations

a) Closed circle, facing center

b) Closed circle, facing CCW

c) Line or open circle, facing CCW

d) Line or open circle, facing center

e) Scatter Formation

2) Couple Formations

a) Single circle of couples facing center

b) Single circle, partners facing

c) Double circle, partners facing, men with backs to center

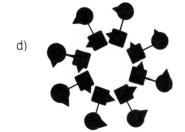

Double circle, partners
side by side, facing CCW

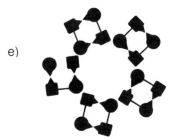

Sicilian Circle: double circle,
couple facing couple

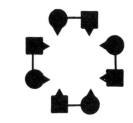

Four couple square or
quadrille formation

3) Longways or Contra Formations

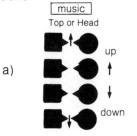

a)

Line of men facing line
of women

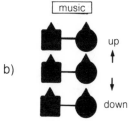

b)

Partners side by side,
facing up or down

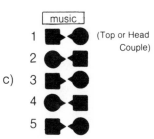

c)

Lines alternating men and
women, partners facing,
actives crossed over.
Actives 1, 3, 5,
Inactives 2, 4, 6

4) Trio Formations

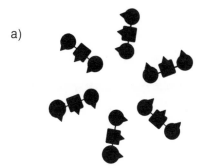

a)

Trios in 'Wheelspoke'
Formation, facing CCW

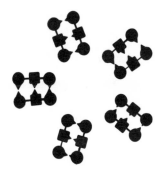

b)

Trios in Sicilian
Circle Formation

c)

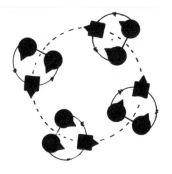

Circle of trios in
triangular handhold

Note: The previous diagrams illustrate only few of the most widely-used dance formations. When planning a series of folk dance lessons, variety in formation and type of dance can increase interest and enjoyment. The total number of students and the proportion of men to women are also crucial factors in the choice of dance formations. Students should be held accountable (in terms of evaluation) only for those positions and formations actually experienced in the particular dances learned.

F. Dance Handholds and Positions

1. Line or Circle Handholds

a) "V" Position   Arms down and straight

b) "W" Position   Hands joined, elbows bent, usually right hand turned up to support neighbor on right, left hand palm down

c) "T" or Shoulder Hold   Elbows straight, hands resting lightly on neighbors' near shoulders

d & e) Front or Back
Chain or
Basket Hold

Arms opened wide, holding
hands of people on other
side of immediate neighbors

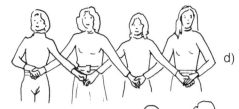

d)

e)

f) Little Finger
Hold

Usually "W" hold (elbows
bent) with little fingers
hooked loosely

f)

2. Couple Positions

a) Ballroom:
Social Dance or
Closed Position.

b) Open or Couple
Position or
Inside
Handhold

Man usually 'supports' the
woman, holding his hand
palm up so that she can
place her hand in his with
her palm down.

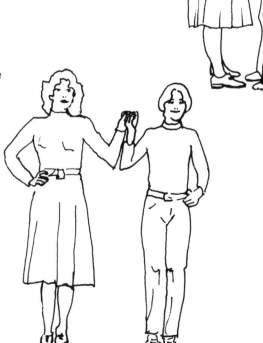

c) Two-Hand
   Position

Men usually hold woman's
hands with man's palm up,
woman's down

d) Elbow Hook

May be with right or left
elbows

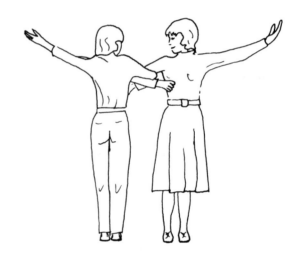

e) Shoulder-
   Waist Position

f) Varsouvienne
   Position

g) Banjo or Sidecar Position
   or Swing Position, right
   hips adjacent

h) Western Promenade
   Skater's or Front Cross
   Position

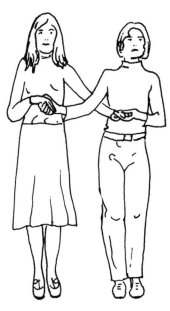

i) Conversation
   or Open
   Position

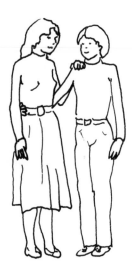

Note: The previous sketches illustrate only a few of the most commonly-used handholds and positions. Each dance should be checked for the specific handholds or positions which are ethnically appropriate, and the position of the outside or free arms should be clarified as well, if possible.

1. In general, any handholds or positions should be *mutually* supportive, firm, but not uncomfortable.
2. In any arm position where the arms are raised and resting on a partner or neighbor, the dancers should use their own muscular effort to support their own arms rather than "hanging" or leaning on neighbors or partners.
3. It is often more comfortable to learn a step pattern individually or joined in a "V" handhold at first, if the appropriate hold is a tiring one. However, once the step is learned, the correct handhold should be used.
4. Handholds in twisting dances or those using under-the-arch figures must be particularly loose and flexible to avoid twisting the wrist or arm.
5. Adjustments should be made, if necessary, to achieve a more comfortable and efficient position when partners or neighbors differ drastically in height or weight. Some line positions may be more comfortable if people of a similar height are grouped together. Comfort will aid in the enjoyment of the dance, but embarrassment should be avoided.

Chapter Three
Skill Development and Teaching Techniques

A. Introduction

Folk dance, at least in Western cultures, is a movement activity primarily using *locomotor* (traveling) types of movement which may be patterned rhythmically, dynamically and/or spatially. It is usually a *group* activity in which one person's movements must be coordinated in different ways with those of a partner or others in the group. A third aspect of traditional dance forms is that they often involve learning, memorizing and performing an *organized sequence* of movement events, frequently structured in relation to a specific melody.

B. General Teaching Techniques

The fundamental locomotor skills as well as the traditional step patterns should be practiced individually first, without music, then put to music at a slowed-down tempo. If the step is done with a partner, it should next be practiced in couples and the music gradually brought up to the proper tempo. Finally, it should be put into the particular sequence of the dance which is being learned. With a complex dance structure, one phrase should be learned at a time, then combined with the next until the total structure is complete.

The initial presentation and practice can be organized spatially in several ways:

1. Arrange the students in a circle formation so that they can travel continuously in one direction while they are practicing. The instructor, standing in the center, should demonstrate the step several times facing different directions, so that all the students can see it at various angles. If possible, use assistant demonstrators standing at various points inside the circle so that all students can follow the person directly in front of them rather than attempting to mirror the instructor if he or she is facing them.

2. For couple practice, a free scatter formation may be used also, with the instructor observing from the side of the room or moving through the group to help those who have problems.

3. For steps which are primarily done in place or moving toward the center and/or back, the group can be arranged in rows with the instructor demonstrating in front facing the same direction as the students. If there are several rows, the instructor or assistants should stand in front of each row at some point, or if there are only two rows, the instructor may turn the group to face the opposite wall and move to stand in front of the new forward row.

C. Folk Dance Skills

SKILL	DESCRIPTION	TEACHING TECHNIQUES AND OBSERVATION POINTS
1. Over-all Coordination Skills	There are several aspects of movement coordination which are particularly important in the skillful execution of any type of folk dance movement :	1. The ability to control and direct the expenditure of *energy* so that one's body moves in the appropriate direction with the appropriate degree of force. 2. The ability to control the *timing* of this exertion of force so as to produce the correct rhythmic movement patterns and synchronize them with the externally-dictated timing of a piece of music. 3. The ability to control one's *balance* in stationary types of movement and also locomotor movements which require more complex patterns of loss and re-establishment of balance.

2. Specific Motor Skills

Specific technical or motor skills required in folk dance are of two types

1. Skill in performing the fundamental types of locomotor steps involving single or double weight changes, or non-weight change steps.
2. Technical or motor skills in performing traditional step patterns or *combinations* of these different types of weight change, in their most basic form (facing and traveling in a single direction) and at a higher skill level, while turning with a partner.

3. Fundamental Locomotor Skills

Human beings can transfer weight by walking, running, leaping, hopping or jumping (excluding the use of hands, or other parts of the body). However, there are several two-part combinations of the above locomotor skills, some with a characteristic rhythmic or spatial aspect, which occur so frequently and naturally that they are usually included in any list of fundamental types of locomotion: galloping, sliding, step-hopping, skipping.

Note: There are many ways of styling these fundamental locomotor skills. The elements listed in the descriptions below are the *essential* characteristics which define each type of weight change in its usual form. Because these basic forms of locomotion are the "building blocks" of even the most complex phrases of folk dance movement, it is important to be clear and specific as to their definition.

a) Single Weight-Change Skills

Skill Diagram

Walk

Dynamics: Normally unaccented, economical use of energy.

Step:	Walk	Walk	Walk	Walk
Timing: *even rhythmically*				
Weight Transference:	R	L	R	L

Spatial Factors: Can be in any direction.

Normal Walk

1. A rhythmically-even transfer of weight from one foot to the other while one foot remains in contact with the floor.
2. One step, or walking action, equals one weight transfer.
3. In a natural walk with a fairly long stride, the heel touches first, then the weight is transferred gradually to the ball of the foot which pushes off to initiate the next step.

"Dance" Walk

1. A "dance" walk with a more controlled landing onto the ball of the foot with the heel barely touching, a shorter-than-normal length of stride, and a slightly greater-than-normal body lean forward (from the ankles), will achieve a smoother flow of movement in figure dances which require many changes of direction.

Couple Walk

1. A couple walk in a closed position where the man's and woman's feet have to move between or beside each other must be done with feet in a parallel rather than a turned-in

or turned-out foot position.

Backward Walk	1. In a backward walk, shorter steps should be taken and the weight should be maintained over the supporting leg for a longer length of time until a secure base is established for the weight shift.
Common Faults:	1. Stride too long 2. Knees and ankles too stiff 3. Weight too far back on heels 4. An unbalanced carriage of the upper body
Teaching Techniques	See general discussion pages 12 and 13.

Run

Skill Diagram

Dynamics: More forceful than walk, but normally unaccented.

Step: Timing: *even* but faster than walk	Run	Run	Run	Run
Weight Transference:	R	L	R	L

Spatial Factors: Into-the-air motion, combines upward motion with movement in any horizontal direction

Normal Run	1. Like the walk, a normal run is an even transfer of weight from one foot to the other, but, because of greater force exerted upward by the extension of the driving leg, there is a brief period in which both feet are off the ground and the body is propelled through the air.
Direction of Force Exertion	1. Determines how high or long each running step is, but normally, the steps are moderate in size and one is more aware of running as an on-going series of steps.
Landing	1. The landing in a dance run is onto the ball of the foot first. 2. Control of the rolling foot action which lowers the heel to the floor and bending the knee and ankle will help absorb the shock of landing.
Body-lean	1. The body-lean forward from the ankles is greater than in walking.
Common Faults:	1. Lean too far forward, making it difficult to stop 2. Landing on the heel and/or stiff-legged 3. Greater than necessary exertion of force 4. Stride too long
Teaching Techniques	See general discussion pages 12 and 13.

Leap

Skill Diagram

Dynamics: Even more forceful than run. One leap can be used as an accent.

Step:	Leap	Leap	Leap	Leap
Timing: *even* but slower than run				
Weight Transference:	R	L	R	L

Spatial Factors: Into-the-air motion.
Height or distance can be emphasized in a single leap.

Series of Leaps

1. A series of leaps can be thought of as large (high and/or long), slow runs.
2. These are not found very frequently in recreational folk dances.

Single Leap

1. A single leap however, is often used in combination with one or more walking or running steps to create an accent.

Mechanics of Leaping

1. For the mechanics of leaping, see the RUN description.

Common Faults:

1. Landing on the heel first
2. Landing with the knee locked.
3. Too great an extertion of force upward will consume more time than allowed by the music.

Teaching Techniques

See general discussion pages 12 and 13.

Hop

Skill Diagram

Dynamics: Forceful, strenuous if in a series.

Step:	Hop	Hop	Hop		Hop	Hop	Hop
Timing: *even*							
Weight Transference:	R	R	R	or L	L	L	

Spatial Factors: Into-the-air motion, dominantly upward. Other horizontal directions can be added to the upward motion.

Hop

1. The word "hop" is often used in a general sense to describe any movement in which the body is propelled into the air for an instant.
2. In dance, one hop is defined more specifically as a movement which takes off from one foot, lifts the body into the air and lands on the *same* foot.
3. In order to transfer weight to the other foot, another form of locomotion such as walk, run or leap must be added.

Take-off and Landing	1. Hopping requires a strong straightening action of the knee and ankle during the take-off since one leg must lift the entire body weight.
	2. The hip, knee and ankle joints must bend slightly on landing in order to soften the impact of the fall and the body should be securely balanced over the supporting leg.
	3. If the weight is too far forward, the tendency will be to leap onto the other leg.
	4. The total body balance may also be affected by the position of the free leg relative to the trunk on the take-off. If the knee is lifted in front to aid in the upward thrust, the body will compensate by shifting the weight back slightly and a balanced landing will be easier.
Hopping Sideward	1. In a series of side hops with heel clicks, if the body travels to the right side while hopping on the left foot, it will help to lean slightly to the left with the upper body so as to counter-balance the clicking action of the right leg.
Common Faults:	1. Failure to use a preparatory flexion before the extension into the take-off
	2. Landing stiff-legged
	3. Exerting force at an angle which will throw the body off balance.
Teaching Techniques	See general discussion pages 12 and 13.

Skill Diagram

Jump

Dynamics: Forceful.

Step:	Jump	Jump	Jump	Jump
Timing: *even, if in series*				
Weight Transference:	LR	LR	LR	LR

Spatial Factors: Into-the-air motion, dominantly upward. Other horizontal directions or a turn may be added to the upward thrust.

Jump	1. A jump is defined as a movement which may take off from one or both legs, but which lands on two legs simultaneously.
	2. As in the leap and the hop, it requires a preparatory bending before the strong straightening action which lifts the body into the air.
	3. Many styles of jumps are possible depending on the shape and action of the legs while in the air and the landing position of the feet.
Common Faults:	See HOP

Teaching Techniques	See general discussion pages 12 and 13.

Note: Because of the potential for knee and foot damage by an incorrect landing, vigorous jumps, leaps and hops should not be done without a preparatory warm-up. Proper foot-leg action should be stressed.

b) Double Weight-Change Skills

Note: The potential technical problems which may occur are usually the same as those discussed in the primary single weight-change forms of locomotion. In the rhythmically uneven patterns, timing is probably the most common difficulty. For teaching techniques, see the general discussion pages 12 and 13.

Skill Diagram

Gallop

Dynamics: May be vigorous. Long step accented more strongly.

Step:	or	Walk Run	Leap Run	Walk Run	Leap Run
		Long	Short	Long	Short
Timing: *uneven* faster than walk					
Weight Transference:		R	L	R	L or opp. ftwk.

Spatial Factors: Usually performed traveling forward. Either height or distance may be emphasized.

Gallop

1. A gallop can be thought of as a longer (time-wise) walking step plus a shorter leap.
2. Usually, the walk is twice as long as the leap.
3. However, if the driving leg is strongly extended on the take-off the knees lifted high and the steps fairly long, the body will rise into the air and both locomotor steps will become runs, unevenly timed.
4. The longer step or run is more strongly accented, and the take-off is always off the same foot.
5. To change lead foot, a step-hop must be added.

Skill Diagram

Slide

Dynamics: First step usually accented more strongly.

Step:	Walk	Leap	Walk	Leap
	Long	Short	Long	Short
Timing: *uneven*				
Weight Transference Traveling to Right:	R	L	R	L
				(opp. ftwk. traveling to left)

Spatial Factors: Sideways motion. Following foot closes beside lead foot.

Slide	
	1. A slide (also called a "sashay," "chassez," or "slipping step") is normally experienced as a sideward type of gallop, that is, a step-leap or uneven run to the right side with the right foot leading, or to the left side with the left foot leading.
	2. The quality of the movement is different from a gallop because of the physical position of the legs. The following leg tends to move into a closed position *beside* the leading leg by being *drawn* along the floor rather than lifted into the air.

Common Faults:	
	1. When working with any sideward locomotor movement, be sure that the front or back of the trunk does not turn to face the direction of motion.
	2. The side of the hip and shoulder should lead.

Step-Hop

Skill Diagram

Dynamics: Evenly accented, usually forceful.

Step:	Walk (step)	Hop	Walk (step)	Hop
Timing: *even* rhythmically				
Weight Transference:	R	R	L	L

Spatial Factors: Usually done traveling forward. May be done with crossing steps sideward, or turning.

Step-Hop	See SKIP

Skip

Skill Diagram

Dynamics: First step usually accented more strongly.

Step:	Walk (step)	Hop	Walk (step)	Hop
	Long	Short	Long	Short
Timing: *uneven* usually two to one				
Weight Transference:	R	R	L	L

Spatial Factors: Usually done traveling forward or turning.

Skip	
	1. The evenly-timed step-hop, is not as natural a type of locomotion for most people as an unevenly-timed step-hop or skip. This may be due to the longer length of time allowed for the preparatory flexing or spring action which precedes the thrust upward in a skip or the shorter time the body must remain in the air before landing at the completion of a hop. However, except for the timing the two are identical.
	2. Students should be clear as to the distinction between them and able to perform both with rhythmic accuracy.

c) Non Weight-Change Skills

1. In addition to different types and combinations of *locomotor* movements, there are other movements which are an important part of a folk dance "vocabulary." These might be thought of as "gestures" or accents, and they include foot and leg movements as well as movements of the hands, arms, and, occasionally, the head and trunk as well.

2. For many people, particularly those brought up in Western cultures, movements of the hands, arms and upper body may be difficult when synchronized, or, particularly, when non-synchronous, with accompanying footwork patterns. With the exception of simple clapping and finger-snapping movements which can be performed and enjoyed by everyone, most arm and body movement patterns require more advanced coordination skills.

3. Leg and foot gestures, on the other hand, play an important role in movement patterns of all levels of difficulty. Although they do not serve functionally to help the body move through space, they are distinct movements which occupy one or more beats in a rhythmic pattern and often provide dynamic or spatial accentuation.

   These gestures include: stamping (when the stamping foot is lifted after the stamp rather than taking weight); touching the heel, sole, or the ball of the foot, or pointing the toe; lifting the free leg with the knee bent, or swinging it across in front or behind the supporting leg; kicking the free leg in the air in various directions with different leg and foot shapes; slapping the foot down on the floor with the leg straight; and many others.

   The supporting leg can "gesture" as well by bending and straightening the knee, or adding a bounce between each step, rising up to the toe, and so on.

4. If the instructor will cue these movements verbally in sequence with the weight-change locomotor steps, it will be easier for the dancer to place them properly in the total rhythmic and movement phrase. For example:

4. Traditional Locomotor Step Patterns

The fundamental locomotor coordinations or steps have been combined into infinite patterns by various ethnic cultures. Some of the most popular and widely used ones are described below.

a) Basic Form

(Traveling and Facing a Single Direction)

Touch-Step

Skill Diagram

Dynamics: Almost even accentuation but weight change on step tends to create a slight syncopated accent.

Step:	Touch	Step	Touch	Step
Timing: *even* 4/				
Weight Transference:	R	R	L	L

Spatial Factors: Touch can be in place, forward, diagonally or to the side, depending on styling and personal choice. Touch can be with heel, sole or ball of foot. Step can be done in place or traveling.

Double Weight-Change Pattern

1. This double weight-change pattern and its reverse (step-touch), are currently familiar steps due to the popularity of disco dancing and the revival of swing and the Lindy step.

Common Faults:

1. The Touch-Step can play an important role in developing awareness of the difference between retaining weight on the supporting leg while touching the other foot and transferring weight via a walking step to the *opposite* leg.
2. This becomes an important distinction in such traditional steps as the Two-Step and the Waltz.
3. In many individual Novelty dances, the Touch-Step is done in place, requiring the maintenance of balance over the supporting leg.
4. Since the step is a small one beside the other foot, it does *not* require as much control over the loss of balance as a larger traveling step would.

Schottische

Skill Diagram

Dynamics: Vigorous. Strong accent on first step, light accent on third.

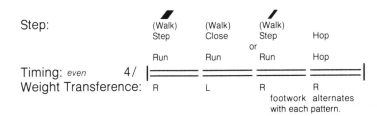

Step:	(Walk) Step	(Walk) Close	(Walk) Step or	Hop
	Run	Run	Run	Hop
Timing: *even* 4/				
Weight Transference:	R	L	R	R

footwork alternates with each pattern.

Spatial Factors: Can be done forward, sideways; crossing in front or behind or closing on second step, backward or turning.

Styling: Varied. May be done running lightly, up on the balls of the feet, or walking in a heavier, more sedate fashion with smaller, flat-footed steps; free leg may swing straight forward during the hop, or be lifted slightly underneath body. Hop may vary from a slight lift to a higher movement.

Steps

1. The schottische step notated above is a widely-used traditional pattern found in many cultures with many differences in styling.
2. The timing is regular; variety is achieved in the locomotor step pattern which combines walking (or running) and hopping and in the spatial figures which can be performed using this step.
3. The German-Scandinavian "Schottische" *dance* structure consists of *two* schottische steps *plus* four even step-hops, arranged in various fixed-sequence dance patterns, or done free style in couples with figures decided upon by the man.

Common Faults:

1. Couple schottische dances often involve a couple turn, requiring more advanced skills in turning with a partner.
2. In the running schottische step, too great a forward body lean may cause the dancer to leap rather than hop on the fourth count if he or she fails to pull back to a vertical balance before the upward take-off into the hop.
3. In the walking step-close-step-hop schottische, the closing action of the second step may be performed incorrectly as a touch rather than a step.
4. If students have not had previous experience with the Two-Step, it may be preferable to start with the running version to avoid this problem.
5. Since the schottische is vigorous, the instructor should be aware of the energy limitations of the students and intersperse pauses for discussion or clarification.

Suggested Teaching Progression:

1. Listen to the music, feel the regular underlying beat grouped in measures of four.
2. At a fairly slow, but even tempo, take three open forward walking steps and pause or hold on the fourth count.
3. Still at a fairly slow tempo, take three open walking steps. Lift or bounce up to the toe of the supporting leg on the fourth count -- "walk, walk, walk, lift."
4. Increase the tempo gradually until the walk changes to a run and the lifting to a hop. Depending upon the style of the dance toward which you are working, a slight leg swing or knee lift forward may help achieve elevation on the hop and shift the body weight back to the vertical. However, if the step is performed in a closed line or circle formation, too large a leg gesture may endanger neighboring dancers. Leg swings or lifts should be *low*, not Can Can kicks!

If the Schottische *dance* is to be performed, add the following steps to the above progression:

5. Teach or review even step-hops.
6. Have students, all traveling in the same direction, perform a few schottische step patterns, then a few even step-hops, learning to alternate back and forth between the two patterns without being constrained to a specific number of repetitions.
7. Have students alternate between *two* schottische step patterns and *four* step-hops--that is, the traditional combination.
8. Do the forward schottische dance pattern in *couples*, standing in open side-by-side position, facing CCW, inside hands joined. Use *opposite* footwork if required in dance--

that is, inside people (men) start *left,* outside people (women) start *right.* Opposite footwork is only *essential* if the dance to be worked on involves a couple turn in closed position. It is commonly used in many couple dances however, although some schottische dances in Varsouvienne hold use the same footwork for both partners.

Two-Step

Skill Diagram

Dynamics:

	(Walk)	(Walk)	(Walk)			
Step:	Step	Close	Step	Step	Close	Step
	1	+	2	1	+	2
Timing: *uneven* (QQS)	2/4					
Weight Transference:	R	L	R	L	R	L

footwork alternates with each pattern

Spatial Factors: May be done forward, sideward or turning.

Styling: May be slow, smooth and gliding or lively and bouncy.

Two-Step

1. The Two-Step (which has *three* weight changes) is a widely used pattern found in such diverse types of dance as Armenian dances and American round dances.
2. It uses only a walking step but has rhythmic and spatial variety.
3. There is a running version of the Two-Step as well:

2/4 | Leap Run | Run |

Common Faults:

1. Even though the Two-Step is frequently used, it can present difficulties for some beginners because the steps are spatially uneven--the second progresses only half the distance of a normal step, stepping into a closed position beside the other foot.
2. There is a tendency to perform this closing movement as a touch rather than a transfer of weight.
3. The smooth styling requires a continuous flow of movement.
4. Rather than "freezing" on count four, the following leg should be brought slowly through to a forward position to lead off the next step pattern.

Suggested Teaching Progression

1. Work on the rhythmic aspect first, all students traveling in a forward direction--that is, do three natural, *open* walking steps in the uneven timing: "Walk, walk, walk, pause."
2. Facing *center,* do three steps sideways without crossing behind or in front--that is, moving in a CCW direction; R,L,R, (pause), then, moving to the left side or in a CW direction; L,R,L, (pause). The second step will naturally become a step into closed position and, because the third step is more easily taken with the leg nearest the direction of motion, the weight transference onto the closing leg also occurs automatically.
3. Returning to motion in a forward direction around the circle, emphasize that the second step should also be a

closing step in the forward Two-Step. Practice: "Step-close-step (pause)."

4. Starting slowly, gradually increase the tempo to a fairly lively one. At this point, the closing action of the second foot usually becomes a sliding one. The foot retains a slight contact with the floor while being drawn forward.

5. If three weight changes occur, the opposite foot will lead into the next pattern. Students can check their own footwork to be sure this is happening.

Heel-Toe Polka

Easy version

Skill Diagram

Dynamics: Energetic. Accentuation relatively even.

Step:	Touch R Heel	Touch R Toe	Step (Walk)	Close (Walk)	Step (Walk)

Timing: *uneven* 2/4
Weight Transference: L   R   L   R

(footwork alternates with each pattern.)

Spatial Factors: Done forward or sideways.

With a Polka Step:

Step:	Touch R heel while hopping L	Touch R toe while hopping L	Hop L	Step Walk	Close Walk	Step Walk

Timing: *uneven* 2/4
Weight Transference: L   L   L   R   L   R

(footwork alternates with each pattern)

Spatial Factors: As in Easy Version above.

Description

See Polka below.

Polka

Skill Diagram

Dynamics: Energetic.
Unevenly accented.

One polka step

Step:	Hop "a"	Step one	Close and	Step two (and)

Timing: *uneven* 2/4
Weight Transference: L   R   L   R

(Footwork alternates with each pattern.)

Spatial Factors: May be done forward or sideways, or turning.

Styling: Lively, light and bouncy.

Polka Steps

1. The *heel-toe polka* can easily be done after the two-step has been mastered by doing a heel, then a toe touch, then a step-together-step (two-step). However, more of a polka flavor may be added if, while touching the heel, then the toe, one simultaneously hops twice on the supporting leg, then adds a third, shorter hop with the same leg just before the two-step; that is, one heel touch, hopping, one toe touch, hopping, plus one polka step.

2. Like the schottische, the traditional Bohemian-German-Scandinavian *polka* step has three steps and one hop, but the polka has a *shorter* hop at the *beginning* of the movement pattern. Musically, this hop comes at the end of the preceding bar on the last third of the second beat of the measure. The strong downward accent comes after the landing from the hop, on the first step of the two-step, coinciding with the accent at the beginning of each measure. The third step of the two-step is slightly shortened to allow room for the beginning up-beat hop of the next polka step.

3. The polka is a more complex step with variety both in its locomotor coordinations, the rhythmic patterning, and dynamics as well. A polka can also be danced to 6/8 meter music using a continuous "short-long" timing. However, most folk polkas are in the 2/4 meter.

Suggested Teaching Progression

One approach to teaching the polka is as follows:

1. Clap or "say" the polka rhythm to the music.
2. Start with a forward two-step, if mastered, and try to put a short lift or hop in front of it: "Step-close-step....." "Lift-step-close-step..."
3. Have the students practice *only* the quick hop and the first strong step of the two-step: "hop-*step*," then try to add the second and third steps of the two-step: "hop-STEP-close-step..." making the hop shorter and the last step slightly longer than the previous two steps.
4. Start slowly, concentrating on one step pattern. Pause, then do another. Then do polka steps in series, gradually speeding up.
5. When dancing a continuous series of polka steps, the student unfamiliar with the music may find it easier to begin with an ordinary two-step rather than starting with the hop on the upbeat before the musical phrase: "Step-close-step...hop-step-close-step/hop-step-close-step..." and so on.
6. A 6/8 polka can be taught initially with a long-short timing as a slide or gallop plus a skip, if one ignores the start on the upbeat hop. However, at some point, a transition should be made to the traditional pattern *starting* with the hop.

Note: There are many ethnic cultures which have a step they call "Polka." These steps are not necessarily identical with the polka just described, in fact some are what we would label as a Two-Step since they do not have any hop. Dance descriptions should clarify the actual foot work and timing of the specific step required, but unfortunately, some do not.

Skip Change Of Step

Skill Diagram

Dynamics: Energetic. Unevenly accented.

Step:

Timing: Reel or 2/4 time *even* and fast   Hop Step Close Step

Weight Transference: L   R   L   R
(lead foot alternates)

Spatial Factors: Only done traveling forward or turning.

Styling: Lively but precise, done high on balls of feet. Body erect, toes pointed, legs and feet turned out. Forward leg extended when reaching forward.

Skip Change of Step

1. The Scottish Skip Change of Step is closely related to the polka as far as the kind and number of basic locomotor steps involved.
2. It varies, in its rhythmic aspect, from the traditional Bohemian-German-Scandinavian polka.
3. The Skip Change of Step in 2/4 Reel time, gives all steps an *equal* timing.
4. In 6/8 Jig time, the short-long-short-long timing is the same as the 6/8 polka.

Common Faults:

1. The most challenging aspect of the step is the elegant and precise Scottish styling.
2. The Skip Change of Step may be taught in a progression similar to the polka progression above.
3. If the polka has been mastered previously, simply demonstrate it, indicate the difference in timing (if in 2/4 meter) and practice to the music.

Pas De Basque

Skill Diagram

Dynamics:

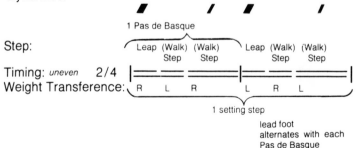

1 Pas de Basque

Step: Leap (Walk) (Walk)   Leap (Walk) (Walk)
Step   Step   Step   Step

Timing: *uneven* 2/4

Weight Transference: R   L   R   L   R   L

1 setting step

lead foot alternates with each Pas de Basque

Spatial Factors: Motion from side to side, in place. First step moves to the side. Second step may cross in front or in back, or step beside the first foot. Third step is in place.

Styling: Scottish style uses turned-out legs, crosses in *front*, on the second skip, and extends the free leg forward, pointed toe just off the floor, on the third step. The weight is transferred onto, and remains, on the ball of the foot, ankles well-stretched.

Setting Step	1. The Pas de Basque, sometimes called the Pas de Bas, or the Setting Step, is used frequently in English, Scottish and Balkan dances. It is closely related to the Two-Step, since it is a three-weight-change pattern in uneven timing.
	2. A Setting Step consists of *two* Pas de Basque patterns, one to the right side and one to the left, done facing and acknowledging another person who is also doing the same.
	3. A Pas de Basque can also be done in 6/8 or Jig time.

Jig time: 6/8

	Leap		Step	Step	

Common Faults:

1. As in the Skip Change of Step, it is the Scottish styling which is the most difficult. (The English styling is more relaxed, and the Balkan styling is sometimes flat-footed with the foot closing beside the other foot on the second beat.)

Suggested
Teaching
Progression

1. Take a small leap to the right side onto the right foot.
2. Take two small steps in place, pausing after the second one: "leap-step-step..."
3. Repeat same pattern to the left side, starting with a leap onto the right foot.
4. Repeat in series, alternating sides, pausing after the third step each time.
5. After the timing and the three weight changes have been experienced, work on the spatial patterning:
   a) A leap to the *side*
   b) A step *crossing* in *front* (if appropriate)
   c) A step *back* in place
      Note: It is the *second* weight change which crosses, not the first.
6. If required for the dance, work on Scottish styling, particularly the free leg extension forward on the third step.

Waltz

Skill Diagram

Dynamics:

Step: Walk Step   Walk Step   Walk Step

Timing: *even* 3/4
Weight Transference: R   L   R
(or opposite footwork)
lead foot
alternates with each
pattern

Spatial Factors: May be done traveling forward, backward, turning, or in place, using the "Box Step" (forward, side, close, back, side, close). Slight dipping (on ct. 1) and rising action (by ct. 3) creates a smoothly lilting change of level. Third step *closes* beside other foot.

Styling: Varied. For example, a peasant or running waltz may be done vigorously with a strongly accented first step. A German-Austrian Laendler-type waltz has an even, flat-footed quality and uses shorter steps and minimal dip.

Forward or Backward Waltz

1. The forward or backward waltz is a simple pattern as far as timing and types of locomotion are concerned, since it consists only of three, evenly-timed walking steps.
2. There is a slight dip on the accented first step, followed by a slight lift to the balls of the feet on the second and third beats.
3. A true waltz step also has the closing step (taking weight), on the third or last step of each group of three, in contrast to the two-step which closes on the second beat.

Common Faults:

1. Moving to the smooth but lilting quality of a *triple* rhythm is a new and different experience for many.
2. As well, the dipping and lifting action requires a balanced posture with slightly more forward lean from the ankles than a normal standing position.
3. Before a turning waltz step is attempted (particularly the fast half-turn clockwise which is commonly used in European folk dances) the closing action on ct. 3 must be mastered and the common tendency to dance a waltz-time two-step corrected.

Suggested Teaching Progression

1. Listen to the music. Feel the grouping into three even basic beats per measure and the stronger accentuation of the first beat.
2. Have the students exaggerate the accent by leaping or stamping (taking weight) on the first beat of each measure; "*oom*-pa-pa," running or walking the second and third beats in a natural open manner.
3. Point out that the leaping or stamping foot alternates with each measure.
4. When the feeling for the metrical grouping of three even beats is established, do a slight knee bend or dip on the first accented step rather than a vigorous leap or stamp and rise gradually to the balls of the feet on counts two and three (still using open steps).
5. Work on the closing, shorter step on count three, making certain that the three weight changes are still being maintained and that the third movement does *not* become a touch.

Skill Diagram

Mazurka Step

Dynamics: Usually energetic. Secondary accent on ct. *2*.

Step:	Walk	Walk	Hop
Timing: *even* 3/4	R	L	L
Weight Transference:			or reverse footwork

Note that lead foot does *not* alternate.

Spatial Factors: May be done in a forward or sideways direction.

Styling: Varied.

Mazurka Pattern

1. The mazurka step, like the waltz, is a pattern done to music in a *triple* rhythm, but unlike any step pattern described thus far, it is a pattern which does *not* use alternating footwork.
2. The first step may be styled as a strong stamping step or a forward glide.
3. The second step is sometimes a 'cut' step; the following foot closing so as to displace the lead leg which is then extended sharply forward.
4. During the hop which occurs on the third beat, the free leg is sometimes bent sharply at the knee from its straight position during ct. 2 or it may be lifted vertically with the knee slightly bent.
5. A mazurka step with a transposed locomotor pattern also exists: on ct. 1, there is a lift (or sweep across) of the free leg while the supporting leg does a lift or hop, cts. 2 and 3 are two walking steps.

Common Faults:

1. As with any pattern containing a hop, there may be a tendency for some people to leap.
2. Emphasize that the weight should be balanced and maintained over the foot taking the second step.
3. Progress forward is achieved during the first two steps.
4. The body bends forward slightly into the accented first step, then straightens on the second step, pulling back to achieve a vertical balance so that the hop can be done in place, the force of the take-off being directed upward.

Suggested Teaching Progression

1. Start slowly. Practice doing two walking steps and one hop. Have students check that their lead foot is always the *same*.
2. Gradually increase tempo and energy output, accenting the first step more strongly.
3. Work on body lean and pull-back if appropriate.
4. Work on particular styling required.

Skill Diagram

Bleking Jump

Dynamics: Vigorous

Step:

Timing: *various* 2/4

Weight Transference:

or 4/4

Spatial Factors: Feet land in forward-back stride position. Forward foot alternates. Done in place.

<table>
<tr><td>Jumping Step
Pattern</td><td>1. This is a type of jumping step, in place, which is performed in various rhythmic patterns depending on the dance.
2. Although the name is Swedish, it is found in the dances of many countries.
3. An initiating knee bend and spring upward precedes the landing on the downbeat of the music, at which time, both feet land simultaneously in a forward-backward stride position.
4. The following jumps alternate the forward and backward legs.
5. Sometimes the weight is evenly distributed between the two feet. However, more usually, most of the weight remains on the back leg, with the forward heel, toe or sole touching depending on the particular styling of the dance.</td></tr>
<tr><td>**Common Faults:**</td><td>1. There may be a tendency to jump and land with the knees stiff or locked.
2. Emphasize the preparatory spring action before the take-off as well as a slight flexing of the knee on the landing to absorb the shock.</td></tr>
</table>

Crossing Step Patterns

a) Side and Close Together

b) Side and Cross-Behind

Skill Diagram

Step: Walk   Walk   Walk   Walk
Timing: *various*
Weight Transference: R   L   R   L   (reverse footwork if moving CW)

Spatial Factors: R Side   Tog.   R Side   Tog.
(Traveling CCW)

or

Walk   Walk   Walk   Touch L

R   L   R
(reverse footwork if moving CW)

R Side   Tog.   R Side   Close
(Traveling CCW)

Step: Walk or Run   Walk or Run   Walk or Run   Walk or Run

Timing: *various*
Weight Transference: R   L   R   L   (moving CCW)
Spatial Factors: Side   Cross Behind   Side   Cross Behind
(When moving CW use opposite footwork)

or

Walk or Run   Walk or Run   Walk or Run   Walk or Run

L   R   L   R   (moving CCW)

Cross Behind   Side   Cross Behind   Side
(When moving CW use opposite footwork)

c) Side and
Cross-Front

Step: Walk   Walk   Walk   Walk
Timing: *various*

	Walk	Walk	Walk	Walk	
Weight Transference:	R	L	R	L	(moving CCW)
Spatial Factors:	Side	Cross Front	Side	Cross Front	

(When moving CW use opposite footwork)

or

	Walk	Walk	Walk	Walk	
	L	R	L	R	(moving CCW)
	Cross Front	Side	Cross Front	Side	

(When moving CW use opposite footwork)

Crossing Step
Patterns

1. Sideways crossing steps may have evolved in ancient times from the need to remain facing and focused on an object of worship (often a tree or a person) as one danced in a circle around it.
2. An infinite variety of crossing step patterns still exist today in line and circle dances which continue to be the dominant form of dance in the Balkans and the Near East.
3. Skill in performing sideways movements is an important factor in mastering the dances of these areas.
4. Movement in a sideways direction can be accomplished by combining sideways steps by the lead foot with steps by the following foot which:
   a) close beside
   b) cross behind
   c) or cross in front of the lead foot.
5. If the next pattern is to be performed in the opposite sideways direction, the last closing step will be done without taking weight, merely touching so that the lead foot closest to the new direction is freed.
6. Crossing patterns may also be initiated by the foot farthest from the direction of motion; "cross-side" as well as "side-cross."
7. The "cross-side" pattern is also known as the Hungarian "downrida" or the square dance "buzz step," while the "side-cross" pattern in Hungary is called the "up" or open rida.
8. A popular combination of side steps with alternating back and front crossing steps is known as the "grapevine step" (see page 42).

Common Faults:

1. In teaching sideways movement which is experienced less frequently in daily life than forward motion, the instructor should emphasize that the front of the body, particularly the chest and shoulders, must remain facing the center.
2. This type of movement will be more comfortable and will look better if the sideways steps are much shorter in length than a normal forward stride.
3. There is a natural tendency for the crossing leg, whether it crosses in front or behind, to bend slightly at the knee, and for the sideways leg action to transfer weight onto a relatively-straight leg. This is part of the styling of many crossing steps.

Grapevine Step

Skill Diagram

Dynamics: First Step accented: ◢ May be smooth or vigorous.

Step: May be walking or running steps, or occasionally step-hops. ◢

Timing: *even* 4/4 | ═ ═ ═ ═ |
Weight Transference: L R L R (Direction-CCW) Opp. ftwk. in CW direction

Spatial Factors: Cross Front Side Cross Behind Side

Spatial Factors: Cross front, side, cross behind, side. Sideways motion, may be done in either a CW or CCW direction. Legs and pelvis may rotate slightly, but arm hold usually keeps the upper body facing the center.

Styling: Various. The Israeli grapevine is often done vigorously with a slight bend of the knee and stamp into the first step coinciding with the metrical accent, and a slight lift or leap into the fourth step. In Greek and Armenian dances, the grapevine patterns are usually smooth, but still done with a flexible spring in the ankles and knees.

Grapevine Step Pattern

1. Combining the various possibilities of sideways movement, the Grapevine Step (also known as the Mayim or Cherkessiya Step in Israeli dances) traditionally is a four-step combination.
2. The step pattern may start on either the side or the crossing phase depending on the dance.

Common Faults:

See discussion in Crossing Step Patterns page 40.

Hora-Hasapikos Step

Skill Diagram

Dynamics: Major accent is not always synchronous with metrical accent.

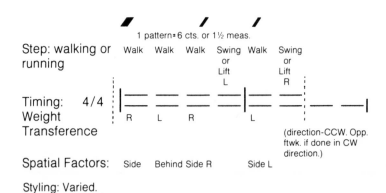

1 pattern = 6 cts. or 1½ meas.

Step: walking or running Walk Walk Walk Swing or Lift L Walk Swing or Lift R

Timing: 4/4 | ═ ═ ═ ═ | ═ ═ — |
Weight Transference: R L R L (direction-CCW. Opp. ftwk. if done in CW direction.)

Spatial Factors: Side Behind Side R Side L

Styling: Varied.

Hora-hasapikos Pattern

1. Because this is one of the most universally-popular patterns throughout the Balkans and Near East, there are many variants and stylings.
2. It may be done smoothly or vigorously, the steps before the swings may be done as jumps, turns may be done on the first two steps of the pattern, extra bounces added, etc..
3. Traditionally, women do this pattern in a more restrained way with lower leg lifts or swings than the men.

Common Faults:

1. See discussion in Crossing Step Patterns above.
2. Individual dance descriptions should be checked as to the specific styling and variations permissible in the context of one particular dance.
3. Because the pattern overlaps the musical meter and the accents are not always synchronous with the musical accents, there is a tendency to let the music pull one off the regular six-beat dance timing.
4. It should be emphasized that the swings or lifts on cts. 4 and 6 take the same length of time as the steps.

Bokazo

(or Hungarian Break Step)

Skill Diagram

Dynamics: Sharp, sudden movements

	Hop	Hop	Jump
Step:			
Timing: *uneven* 4/4			
Weight Transference:	L	L	LR (or opposite footwork)

Spatial Factors: Done in place. Toe of free leg touches in front or across supporting leg (toe turned out) on first hop, touches to the side (toe may be slightly turned in, heel out) on the second hop, and closes beside the other leg on the jump. Heels may click together.

Bokazo Pattern

1. This popular pattern is only one of several types of break step, performed as a flourish to end a dance or musical phrase.
2. The patterns often involve the clicking of boot heels, particularly for the man.

Common Faults:

1. If the heels are to be clicked together sharply, a slight turn-out of the feet on impact will avoid the discomfort of banging the ankle bones together inadvertently.

b) Turning Form Techniques and Teaching Progressions for Traditional Locomotor Step Patterns

There are a number of factors which make turns more difficult, whether they are individual turning versions of basic locomotor steps such as walking, leaping, jumping or hopping, or couple turns which use some of the traditional step patterns discussed earlier.

1. Individual Turning Techniques

Individual turns use:

i) A pivot action; turning with the weight on the ball of one foot with the heel lifted off the floor slightly to decrease the area of friction, or

ii) An air turn in which the body twists or rotates sharply around a vertical axis while in the air, landing either in a jump, leap, or hop. The technical principles involved in the take-off and landing action are the same as in the non-turning forms of locomotion. As well, the muscular maintenance of the body alignment or position is important since the force of the rotation action may tend to throw the body off its vertical axis, making a balanced landing difficult.

2. Partner Turning Techniques

In most couple turns, the axis around which the turning movement rotates is a point *between* the two partners, making it necessary for both partners to use their combined weight cooperatively to swing themselves around. The turning action will be helped by:

1. Keeping one's feet close to one's partner's feet.
2. Holding each other firmly but not bending forward in a "desperation clutch."
3. Using an erect and balanced body posture.
4. Taking steps which are not too large, but, on the other hand, are large enough to carry the couple further in the direction of motion if the turns are half-turns or full turns which progress horizontally around the room.

Dizziness

1. Dizziness is the major stumbling block in learning to do a continuous series of turns skillfully, since many folk dance turns are done at a fast tempo and require a half-turn per step pattern or even, in the case of some Scandinavian turns, a complete rotation.
2. The woman may minimize dizziness by focusing her eyes on something close (such as her partner's face), rather than looking at the walls which will be a whirling blur.
3. The man, however, is responsible for leading and avoiding collisions, and must take continual quick glances at the flow of traffic around him in order to steer the couple into the open spaces.
4. If it is any consolation to the beginner, repetition and practice do seem to increase tolerance in most individuals and the exhilaration of turning, once dizziness has been conquered, is well worth it.

3. Suggested Skill
   Progression for
   Couple Turns

Two-Hand Turn

1. Stand face-to-face with a partner, toes almost touching.
2. Join both hands and lean back so that each is supporting the other's weight.
3. In this position, take small side-steps or sliding steps turning in place.
4. Caution: This requires:
   a) a firm grip
   b) that each partner recover his or her balance by pulling together before letting go after the rotation action has been stopped
   c) that each person *trust* his or her partner!

Elbow-Hook Turn

1. This is done standing side by side facing opposite directions.
2. Be sure there is tension in the hooking arms. Leaning away with the upper body may help.

Walk-Around Turn

(in modified ballroom hold or swing position)

1. The woman leans back slightly against the man's supportive right hand which should be on the woman's back, either at her waist or slightly above, under her left shoulder blade.
2. Steps should be small and partners' feet close together.
3. If the end of the turn requires a transition into a side-by-side position, woman on the man's right, the man must guide the women with his left hand as they open out to help her make the extra half-turn which puts her on his right side both facing the same direction.

Schottische Step-Hop Turn

(in shoulder-waist position)

Woman's Turn

1. Women practice in an individual circle formation without their partners.
2. All face CCW with the weight on the left foot.
3. Ct. 1, step forward on the right foot, ct. 2, hop on it, turning CW one-half turn to land facing CW, ct. 3, step backward in a CCW direction with the left foot, ct. 4, hop on left, continuing to turn CW another half-turn to face CCW again.
4. For practice, continue turning step-hops (always in a CW direction) for a number of revolutions: ("forward-hop-backward-hop")

Man's Turn

1. Men practice in an individual circle formation without their partners.
2. All start facing *CW* with their weight on the *right* foot.
3. Ct. 1, step backward in a CCW direction with the left foot, ct. 2, hop on left making a half-turn CW to face CCW, ct. 3, step forward with right in CCW dirction, ct. 4, hop on R, turning CW a half-turn.
4. Continue turning for a number of revolutions, always turning CW: ("backward-hop-forward-hop").

Couple Turn

1. Combine the actions of Woman's and Man's Turn in a single circle of couples, men with backs to CCW direction, using shoulder-waist hold.
2. Ct. 1, man starts stepping back with left foot, while woman steps forward with her right foot (in CCW direction), stepping between man's feet. Ct. 2, both hop together using a forceful push-off and body twist to swing both of them around. Ct. 3, man steps forward in CCW direction between woman's feet, woman steps backward. Ct. 4, both hop and make a half-turn CW.
3. Continue turning CW for a while, trying to make a complete half-revolution each time so that each is always facing either a CW or CCW direction.
4. To add the turning version of the step-hops to the forward Schottische steps done in side-by-side position, the man must turn to place himself in front of his partner (with his back to CCW direction), during the hop at the *end* of the second schottische step so that he is ready to step backward into the turn.
5. At the same time, he must take shoulder-waist position, placing his hands on her waist so that he can swing her around with him.
6. Turning may be easier now that use can be made of the momentum gained by the forward motion of the schottische steps.

Another approach to the couple step-hop turn would be:

1. Step-hop as a couple in place without turning.
2. Add a slight degree of rotation CW on each hop.
3. Take four step-hops to complete one revolution (that is, make a quarter-turn on each).
4. Make the traditional two revolutions on the four step-hops, turning half-turn each time.

Two-Step Turn Clockwise
(in ballroom hold)

a) Practice in an individual circle formation, all facing center.

1. Do one two-step to the right side; side R, close L (taking weight), side R, hold.
2. Do one two-step to the left side, starting with the free left foot; side L, close R (taking weight), side L, hold.
3. Progress continuously in a CCW direction by turning; do one two-step to the right side as 1. above, but, during the "hold" on the fourth count, lift up to the ball of the right foot and pivot one-half turn to the right (CW) so that everyone's back is to the center, weight still remaining on the right foot. Continue, doing a second two-step to the left side as in 2. above but, because all are facing out, direction of motion will continue in a *CCW* direction. Pivot on the fourth count again, on the left foot, *still turning in a CW direction* to face the center again.

Note: Some dancers will have a tendency to turn to the left or CCW on this turn. This should be checked by the instructor. Continue to do one two-step facing the center and one facing out, always turning in a CW direction or to the right and always progressing in a CCW direction.

b) Practice in a double circle of couples, men with their backs to the center facing their partners.

1. Take ballroom hold and travel in a CCW direction, men starting with the left foot, women with the right, both pivoting CW on the fourth count of each step pattern.

Note: Now that two people are turning around an axis between them, each will describe a scalloped path rather than a straight line as they progress in a CCW direction.
   To help achieve a complete revolution with two two-steps, the man should begin turning on the third count by stepping with his left foot around the outside of his partner's feet rather than directly to the side. The woman steps forward with her right foot between her partner's feet at the same time. During the second pattern when each partner's facing is reversed, the man should step right between his partner's feet, the woman stepping left around the outside. The left foot must turn in (lead with the heel) and the right foot turn out (lead with the toe) on this third step.

2. Turning the shoulders, that is rotating the trunk in the direction of the turn, will aid the pivoting action.

3. In learning the turning two-step, many beginners will tend to do a polka instead because a hop, with its greater force and less friction is easier to execute than a pivot. The difference in movement quality between a smooth, pivoting two-step and a bouncy hop-polka should be made clear, and the appropriate step and timing required for a particular dance indicated.

Couple 2/4 Polka Turn Clockwise
(using either ballroom or shoulder-waist hold)

a) Individual practice in circle formation, all facing center.

1. If the turning two-step has been learned previously, one can simply change the pivot to a hop by exerting more force in an upward direction, using an even timing to practice the same progression as in the two-step above (step-close-step-*hop*)

2. Then make the hop shorter, changing the rhythm to "'ah' one and two (and)," and begin the step pattern with the hop.

b) Couple practice in double circle formation, men with backs to center, couples in ballroom or shoulder-waist position.

1. Start with the weight on the man's right foot and the woman's left.

2. The series of polka steps can be initiated by a hop on the supporting leg without the turn, or it may be easier for beginners to do one plain turning two-step without the hop before going into the hop-step-close-step polka.

3. This avoids having to anticipate the next phrase of the music in order to begin on the up-beat.

6/8 Polka

a) Individual practice all facing center.

1. Side slide in a CCW direction around the circle.
2. Have dancers change the direction of the slide to CW on verbal command.
3. Point out that what many are doing instinctively is to "put the brakes on" with the leading foot during the first step of the final slide, then hop on it so that the left foot is free to lead in a CW direction.
4. Do eight slides each way (7 1/2 plus a hop).
5. Do four each way (3 1/2 plus a hop).
6. Do two each way (side, close, side, hop)
7. Start the pattern in 6. above with the hop performing a sideways 6/8 polka.
8. Do this pattern continuously in a CCW direction by adding a half-turn CW on each hop; "hop, (turning), slide and step"; and so on.
9. If the timing is changed to 2/4, this progression can also be used to teach the 2/4 turning polka.

Couple Turning Waltz Clockwise

1. In contrast to the slow, modern ballroom waltz in which a quarter-turn is often used, the waltz turn found in most folk dances is a fast half-turn CW which progresses CCW around the room at the same time. This demands greater turning skill.
2. In addition, many dances in which this waltz turn is used (for example, Oslo Waltz) are group or circle mixer dances which require that the circle formation be *maintained* while turning in order to move smoothly into the next figure.
3. If a beginning couple do less than one complete revolution every two waltz steps, they will work themselves in toward the center, breaking the circle formation. Continuance of the dance from a broken formation will be difficult for everybody.
4. Because of this problem, a dance such as Bitte Mand i Knibe (Little Man in a Fix) which is in scatter formation may be a more successful choice as an introduction to the turning waltz.

Suggested Teaching Progression

This is a natural and enjoyable progression which teaches the half-turn, learned from Ned and Marian Gault of the University of the Pacific Folk Dance Camp.

a) The Post Waltz

1. Have an even number of men and women stand alternately in a single circle of couples all facing center.
2. Women stand as "posts" and do nothing. Men practice the following progression:
   a) With three steps, starting right, each man turns toward the woman on his right and steps in front of her, facing her squarely with his back to the center.
   b) With three steps, he turns CW, looking her in the eye as long as possible rather than turning his back on her, and steps beside her on her *right* side, backing into the empty space. Everyone is facing the center again, men having progressed one place around the circle CCW.

c) Continue the turning, gradually talking people into a three-beat rhythm: "(1) turn (2) to (3) face; (1) back (2) into (3) place." Point out that, if one starts to turn with the right foot, turning out the toe to complete the turn as much as possible on this first step, stepping to the side with the left foot will bring the body around to stand squarely in front of the woman, then the right foot closes to step in place on the third count. On the second waltz step, the left heel leads around (toe turned in) on the first count, the right steps slightly to the side so that the body faces the center squarely, then the left closes in place on the third count.

d) Do this three-beat pattern to a regular continuous count and then to music.

4. Men stand as "posts" women follow steps 1 through 4 above.

5. Practice with imaginary posts; the women, then the men backing out of the way--that is, one group at a time do the pattern, still making a scallop floor track instead of going straight (*through* the imaginary posts or people).

6. Couple practice in a double circle of couples in closed ballroom hold, men standing with their backs to the center of the circle, facing their partners. The man starts the waltz turn stepping *back* with his *left* foot while the woman steps forward with her right. In a half-turn the couple moves in a CCW direction as they turn CW by progressing further around the circle on the *second* sideward step. The third step is still a closing step. As in the two-step turn, the right foot must step forward *between* the partner's feet.

b) The Box Waltz

Another method of teaching a CW turning waltz is to teach the "box" waltz:

Step:	R	L	R	L	R	L
Timing: 3/4						
Direction:	Fwd.	Side	Close	Back	Side	Close

1. In individual scatter formation, all facing one wall, have everyone practice the box waltz pattern, without turning.

2. In couples, still in scatter formation so that they can orient themselves with the four walls, practice the box waltz, the man starting back left (measure 2 above), the woman forward right (measure 1 above). Do this in place, without turning, then begin to turn in with the left foot when stepping back on the first count, and out when stepping forward right on the first count, so that the couple turns very gradually in a CW direction.

3. Increase the degree of turn for each measure until one revolution is completed in two waltz steps.

4. Practice to fairly slow waltz music and gradually speed up the tempo.

Couple Buzz-Step Turn

a) American
   Square Dance
   Buzz-Step Turn

This turn differs from a) above in several ways

1. This turn is done in "banjo" or "swing" position, the couple standing in ballroom hold with right hips adjacent, outside borders of right feet close to each other, left feet behind right.
2. The foot action is a two-phase one:
   a) A preparatory push-off with the left foot shifts the weight onto the right foot, the right knee bending slightly as it takes weight. Step onto right foot occurs on the strong downbeat of the music.
   b) Phase two - The left foot steps sideways left, leg straight, as the right foot pivots CW.

b) French
   Canadian
   Buzz-Step Turn

1. Partners face each other squarely rather than standing side by side.
2. The right feet are either placed so that the *inside* borders of the feet are adjacent to each other or so that the toes are almost touching.
3. The arm hold is varied--it may be shoulder-waist or shoulder-shoulder-blade, ballroom hold, or several other positions.
4. The left foot steps straight to the side and the action is a pulling one rather than a push-off.
5. The steps are flat-footed and smooth with minimal knee bending and straightening.

Chapter Four
Sample Lesson Plans

The following lesson plans present a suggested progression of skills and dances for Level I. Other dance and progression choices are possible, however. Some of the lessons also suggest different types of teaching material which may be used as enrichment activities to clarify rhythmic concepts and movement skills.

The plans assume a fifty-minute class of approximately thirty students, the use of standard sound equipment, and a good-sized gymnasium-type space. The individual, line, and trio dances are especially adaptable to any ratio of males to females.

In general, each class should consist of:

a) Some type of warm-up and review activity such as practice of individual locomotor steps or step patterns, and/or dancing one or two dances previously mastered.

b) Presentation of new material; skills and concepts which work toward the achievement of specifically-defined objectives.

c) One or several culminating activities, depending on available time. These may be the completion and performance of the dance which embodies the skills and concepts introduced earlier in the lesson, a short period of request dancing during which the students choose those dances they particularly enjoy, or supplementary enrichment activities.

Level I is an introductory unit designed to review the fundamental locomotor skills and to present basic rhythmic concepts and experiences. These must be mastered for successful and enjoyable folk dancing. The dances chosen are popular and simple ones.
Note: See Chapter Five for detailed dance descriptions.

Lesson One - Pata Pata

1. Objectives

By the end of Lesson One, the student should have begun to:

a) Distinguish between weight transfer and non weight transfer.

b) Have learned the terms "touch," "step," "pivot," "scatter formation."

c) Have been introduced to the concept "basic underlying beat," and experienced it in movement.

d) Have learned the individual dance *Pata Pata*, a type of dance and musical sound which is related to familiar disco and jazz music and movement and thus can be an enjoyable introduction to folk dance for most students.

2. Introduction - 10 min.

Roll check, spend the first 10 minutes defining folk dance, discussing dress requirements, explaining the Levels system, methods of evaluation and emphasizing the need to practice and develop movement skills in order to become a *good* dancer.

3. Review

This would be omitted for the first lesson.

4. New Material: Pata Pata - 25 min.

Introduction:

a) Class in individual scatter formation; all face the music, instructor stands in front of students, facing the same direction as they are when demonstrating.

b) Instructor introduces name and country of dance.

c) Instructor plays music, students experience the basic underlying beat by bouncing at the knees, clapping, snapping fingers.

The Dance (see page 59a)

a) Phrase 1: Touch Step - distinguish between non-transfer and transfer of weight.

b) Add phrase 2 to phrase 1: Heel-toe swivel — suggest several simple to more challenging options for student choice.

c) Add phrase 3: Knee twist action

d) Add phrase 4: Kick plus three walks (*minus* turn).

e) Explain length of musical introduction and do dance in non-turning form to the music.

f) If most of the class have mastered this basic step sequence, add the 1/4 pivot turn to phrase 4. Explain repetition of dance facing a different direction each time. Do completed dance to record.

g) If many are having problems either:
1. postpone turning version of dance to Lesson Two and review parts causing technical problems, or
2. have those who have mastered the dance learn the turn and do it to music while instructor works with second group on basic non-turning form.

5. Culmination Activities - 10 min.

a) At blackboard or with chart: Introduce system of rhythmic notation; discuss role of basic underlying beat; diagram using dash symbol: ___ ___ ___ .

b) Put on *Pata Pata* music or use metronome or hand drum. Have students do repeated touch-step patterns individually with any arm gestures or

c) Have students take pencil and paper and create a sequence of walking steps and touches. For example:

S * Walking Step   T * Touch

<u>S</u> <u>T</u> <u>T</u> <u>T</u> <u>S</u> <u>S</u> <u>S</u> <u>T</u>

d) Exchange papers with another student and "read" each other's patterns. Have students check each other for accurate performance of the pattern as written.

e) If time, repeat the dance, *Pata Pata*.

Lesson Two - Fjäskern

1. Objectives

By the end of Lesson Two the student should have:
a) Developed the skill of walking (running) to a basic underlying beat at varying tempos.
b) Developed skill in making a pivot-type half-turn and continuing to walk in a different direction without losing the basic beat.
c) Learned the terms "couple position" or "inside hand hold," "LOD," "RLOD," "walk," "double circle formation."
d) Learned the couple mixer dance, *Fjäskern*

2. Introduction - 5 min.

Roll check and discussion of material to be covered in Lesson Two.

3. Review - 15 min.

Organize class in scatter formation. Review *Pata Pata*, if necessary, adding the 1/4 turn, and review concept of basic underlying beat.

4. New Material: Fjäskern - 30 min.

(see page 60)
a) Organize students in single circle without joined hands, alternating males and females as much as possible. Instructor stands in center.
b) Introduce the dance and terminology for circle directions: "LOD" and "RLOD."
c) Play the slow beginning music for *Fjäskern*. Have individuals face and walk sixteen steps in LOD, starting with left foot, turning to face RLOD on the sixteenth step, one step to each basic beat of the music. Then have them walk sixteen steps in RLOD in the same manner. Discuss definition of "walk."
d) Form double circle, taking neighbor for partner, couples facing LOD. (If there are more males than females, extra males must be phased out at this point, but should observe and be phased in when dance is repeated. Extra females may dance together.)
e) Introduce inside hand hold.
f) Repeat walking and turning pattern, turning toward each other and rejoining hands after turn.
g) Add second phrase (kick and cross-over).
h) Explain musical introduction and do one sequence of dance with music.

i) Explain method of changing partners and do complete dance as a mixer for entire record. Before starting, emphasize that dancers should try to move with basic beat of the music, trying to walk with "Swedish dignity" as long as possible, but running if necessary. (Part of the fun of this dance is the surprise element of increasing speed, which usually causes chaos the first time through. Laugh with it and don't expect perfection).
j) After dance is over, point out the skill challenge of performing the pattern at a very fast speed and explain the meaning of the name *Fjäskern* which is Hurry Scurry.
k) If necessary, review and work on technical problems.
l) Individual practice: Without music, have students walk and gradually accelerate their speed until they are forced to break into a run.

5. Culmination Activity

Repeat the dance *Fjäskern*, emphasizing styling.

Lesson Three - Troika

1. Objectives

By the end of the Lesson Three, the student should have.:
a) Developed skill in running to a regular beat in the music.
b) Learned to control balance when stopping at the end of a series of runs.
c) Learned the rhythmic concepts of "measure" and "phrase."
d) Learned to identify the musical phrasing in *Troika* and to coordinate the dance phrases with the musical phrasing.
e) Learned the terms "trio" and "wheelspoke formation."
f) Learned the dance figures "arches" and "circle left and right."
g) Learned the trio dance *Troika* from Russia.

2. Introduction - 5 min.

Roll check and give introduction to lesson.

3. Review - 10 min.

Warm-up and review dance: *Fjäskern*

4. New Material: Troika — 25 min.

(see page 60)
a) Organize group into trios in wheelspoke formation. Trios may be one male and two females, or any combination of sexes. Introduce dance.
b) Listen to beat of the dance music.
c) Phrase 1: run 16 steps CCW around circle.
d) Phrase 2: add arches figure. Emphasize loose handhold.
e) Add circle left and stamps: emphasize that the circling run continues for 12 counts.
f) Add circle right and either open into line if doing

non-mixer version, or center person forward to next set for the mixer version.

g) Explain musical introduction and do dance.

5. Culmination Activities - 10 min.

a) Introduce rhythmic concepts of measure and phrase.
   i) Diagram basic underlying beat on the blackboard as presented in Lesson One: — — — —
   ii) Indicate divisions into groupings or *measures* of four by using vertical strokes: | — — — — |
   iii) Listen to music and identify melodic phrasing:

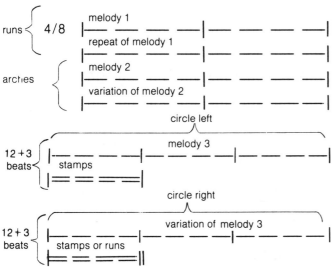

   iv) Have students experience the eight count phrasing by playing the *Troika* music while they run individually eight steps in one direction, then eight steps in another direction, and so on, without pausing or losing the basic beat.

b) Work on technical problem of running and stopping:
   i) Have several students run in a circle and stop suddenly. Have the rest of the students observe their forward lean while running and the pull back to a vertical or balanced position on stop.
   ii) Have students run, individually, anywhere in the room for eight steps and then "freeze," pulling their weight back to a balanced standing position.

c) Repeat the dance, *Troika,* and/or end class by dancing *Pata Pata,* as a cool-down.

Lesson Four -D'Hammerschmiedsgselln

1. Objectives

By the end of Lesson Four, the student should have:
a) Developed skill in performing an unevenly-timed step-hop, or skip, slowly to 3/4 time music.

b) Mastered a hand slap-and-clap coordination sequence and be able to perform it to the music and in the correct relationship to the other three people in the two-couple set.
c) Learned the "star" dance figure.
d) Learned the dance *D'Hammerschmiedsgselln*.

2. Introduction - 5 min.

Check roll and give introduction to lesson.

3. Review - 10 min.

Warm-up and review dance - *Troika*.

4. New Material - D'Hammerschmiedsgselln - 30 min. (see page 61)

a) Teach chorus.
   i) Individual practice of the chorus clap-and-slap pattern.
   ii) In groups of four, facing people practice pattern with each other as two separate pairs. If in a two-couple set, two women practice together, and the two men also, without standing in the cross-over formation.
   iii) In groups of four, standing in the proper formation, practice the pattern with one pair starting one measure later so that the cross-over slaps do not conflict.
b) Teach the three figures — circle, star, large circle.
c) Put the whole dance together.
d) Do dance to music.

5. Culminating Activity - 5 min.

Dance *Pata Pata* as a relaxing cool-down.

Lesson Five - The Crested Hen or Den Toppede Høne

1. Objectives

By the end of Lesson Five, the student should have:
a) Developed skill in performing an evenly-timed step-hop.
b) Understood and experienced the difference between a skip and a step-hop.
c) Developed skill in rotating a circle of three by leaning outward and maintaining tension in the armholds.
d) Used skills learned in *Troika* to perform the under-the-arch figure efficiently using only four step-hops.
e) Learned the dance *The Crested Hen*.
f) Learned the meaning of the dance name and experienced the vigorous and playful quality of movement which is expressive of the Danish character.

2. Introduction - 5 min.

Check roll and give introduction to lesson.

3. Review - 10 min.

Warm-up and review dance: *D'Hammerschmied-sgselln.*

4. New Material: The Crested Hen - 30 min.
(see page 62)

a) Teach even step-hop (point out timing difference from the skip just done in *D'Hammerschmied-sgselln).* Individual practice.

b) In trios, practice 8 step-hops circling CW, 8 circling CCW.

c) Teach and practice arches figure.

d) Put dance sequence together and do dance to music.

e) Discuss dance name and meaning.

5. Culminating Activity - 5 min.

Review *Fjäskern* (another Scandinavian dance with an element of play).

Lesson Six - Gigue aux Six

(Multi-Level Lesson)

1. Objectives

This dance is particularly suitable for use with a class composed of students at various skill levels. Therefore, different objectives must be stated for each of these groups:

Level I Objectives: By the end of Lesson Six, the students:

a) Will be able to perform a side slide in both sideways directions, using a hop to change direction.

b) Will be able to perform a balance step and *walk around* swing.

c) Will have learned the terms "cast-off," "head couple," "longways or contra set."

d) Will have learned the dance *Gigue aux Six* in its basic form and experienced a progressive dance structure.

Level II Objectives: By the end of Lesson Six, in addition to the above objectives, Level II students will have been introduced to one or two simple gigue or clogging steps to be done optionally while standing.

Level III Objectives: By the end of Lesson Six, in addition to the objectives stated for Levels I and II, Level III students will have been introduced to a buzz-step couple swing.

2. Introduction - 5 min.

Check roll and introduce lesson.

3. Review - 10 min.

Warm-up and review dancing from previous lesson.

4. New Material: Gigue aux Six - 30 min.
(see page 62)

For the first fifteen minutes, all students learn basic pattern with walk-around swing.

Then divide class into three groups, by level. Each group must consist of an even number of students, so that all can practice with partners.

Level I group work on direction change in the side slide and the walk-around swing. Review sequence and repeat dance to music if enough for sets of six.

Level II and III groups: Teach gigue steps (see dance description). Leave Level II group to continue practice of these steps individually, doing them slowly at first, then faster and with music.

Level III group (and any of Level II group who wish to try): Teach buzz-step swing, first in a circle, then in couples in shoulder-waist position.

5. Culmination Activity - 5 min.

Have all students form sets of three couples and dance *Gigue aux Six.* Level II and III students may do optional gigue steps while standing in place as inactive couples, Level III couples have the option of doing a buzz-step swing on the turn.

Lesson Seven - La Raspa

1. Objectives

By the end of Lesson Seven, the student should have:

a) Developed skill in performing a Bleking jump.

b) Reviewed skipping or running.

c) Developed ability to create simple dance figures or spatial and partner variations using these locomotor steps.

d) Learned one basic version of the dance *La Raspa.*

2. Introduction - 5 min.

Check roll and give introduction to lesson.

3. Review

Warm-up and review omitted to allow maximum time for creative work.

4. New Material: La Raspa - 35 min.
(see page 63)

a) With students in circle formation or couple scatter, explain definition of *jump* and have students experiment individually with different ways of jumping.

b) Demonstrate Bleking jump and explain rhythmic pattern used in this particular dance. All clap it. Practice jump pattern to music. Two claps in a quick, slow timing can be added during the pause after the three jumps.

c) Add second part: running or small, fast skips. If group is in circle formation, practice running (skipping) 16 steps to left and 16 to right. If in couples, circle L and R with partner.

d) Dance basic version of dance to music.

e) Divide class into small groups of 2, 3, 4 (groups of different sizes produce more varied and interesting patterns) and have each group work out a pattern using spatial, partner or handhold variations to the basic structure. Keep as constants, the Bleking jumps during the first 16 measures, and running or skipping for the second 16 measures.

5. Culminating Activity - 10 min.

Have each group show their pattern (play music only two or three times through the dance, not the whole record for each).

Note: Because this dance is probably not a traditional Mexican ethnic dance, and because several versions using the same steps are already in existence, it is particularly suitable for use as a means of developing student creativity and initiative. Folk dances with more formal, set sequences do not lend themselves to this free approach and their traditional structure should be kept intact.

Lesson Eight - Pljeskavac Kolo

(Multi-Level Lesson)

1. Objectives

This dance is suitable for use with a class composed of students at various skill levels. The objectives for each level are listed below.

Level I: By the end of Lesson Eight, the students:
   a) Will be able to walk in a rhythmic pattern of quick and slow steps, in time with the music.
   b) Will have been introduced to the fundamental elements involved in rhythmic patterning.

Level II: In addition to achieving the objectives listed above, Level II students will be able to dance the variation which uses step-hops as well as walking steps.

Level III: In addition to achieving the objectives listed in Levels I and II above, Level III students will be:
   a) Able to substitute a forward schottische step for the last three walks in the basic pattern.
   b) Have had practice in leading a line in various directions and calling changes while the various dance patterns are being performed.

2. Introduction - 5 min.

Check roll and introduction of lesson.

3. Review - 10 min.

Warm-up and review: *La Raspa.*

4. New Material: Pljeskavac Kolo - 30 min.

(see page 64)

   a) At blackboard: Illustrate and discuss rhythmic patterning. (see page 14).
     i) Review basic beat
     ii) Divide basic beat
     iii) Combine basic beat
     iv) Rhythmic pattern may equal any combination of i, ii, and/or iii In other words, some regular basic beats, some faster beats, some slower beats in a varied pattern.
   b) Put rhythmic pattern of *Pljeskavac* on board:

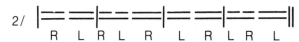

Have students clap and walk this pattern, individually, moving anywhere in the room.
     i) With class in a closed circle, hands joined in "V," instructor in center, teach phrase 1 (above walking pattern, repeated).
     ii) Teach phrase 2 (stamping and clapping).
     iii) Do dance to record.
   c) While Level I students review and practice above sequence, teach Levels II and III the step-hop variation.
   d) Leave Level II to practice, and teach (or review) with Level III the forward schottische step which may be done instead of the last three walking steps. Discuss leading and leading signals.

5. Culmination Activity - 5 min.

In three separate lines, all dancing to the same music, have Level I line do basic pattern (it will be helpful if instructor or one of Level III students leads the line). Level II line will start with the basic pattern and at student leader's signal, change to more vigorous step-hop variation. Level III line will do student leader's choice of any of the three patterns, changing to another at any time. Stop record several times, part way through, so that lines II and II can change leaders, giving as many students as possible the opportunity to lead.

Lesson Nine - Review of Basic Locomotor Steps and Rhythmic Concepts

1. Objectives

   a) To review basic locomotor steps.
   b) To review rhythmic concepts covered and system of notation.
   c) To introduce Level II Folk Dance and the more challenging traditional step patterns which combine several basic locomotor steps and/or vary one step rhythmically.
   d) To have students experience patterning by creating, notating, and performing their own combinations of locomotor steps.

2. Introduction - 5 min.

Check roll and introduction of lesson.

3. 15 min. Review

   a) Review basic forms of locomotion: walk, run, leap, hop, jump, step-hop, skip, gallop, side slide:
     i) Instructor or students demonstrate one basic locomotor step at a time.
     ii) Other students observe, and all discuss the

defining characteristics of each and the difference between them.

b) Review on blackboard the rhythmic concepts covered, using notation system to illustrate them: basic underlying beat, measure, phrase, making longer or shorter beats by dividing or combining basic beats, rhythmic patterning. Students experience concepts by clapping and/or moving.

c) Have students work out a short movement pattern which combines several basic locomotor steps, perhaps including rhythmic variety as well. Have them take pencil and paper and notate their pattern using a visual symbol system such as letters or geometric shapes (better for young children). For example:

W = walk,   R = run,   H = hop,   J = jump

$$4/ \quad \| \underset{R}{\overset{W}{=}} \; \underset{R}{\overset{H}{=}} \; \underset{L}{\overset{W}{=}} \; \underset{L}{\overset{H}{=}} \; | \; \underset{R}{\overset{R}{=}} \; \underset{L}{\overset{R}{=}} \; \overset{J}{\underset{LR}{=\!=}} \| $$

d) Have several students put patterns on blackboard for all to "read" and do.

e) Have students take partners and exchange papers, each "reading," doing and checking the other's performance for accuracy.

f) If time, dance as many dances as possible.

Lesson Ten - Dance

Review dancing and/or hold folk dance party planned by the students.

Chapter Five
Evaluation

Evaluation should be helpful, positive, and presented in such a way that it does not discourage the students, especially those with little or no previous background in dance. The experience of being evaluated can create tension which, in itself, is a major cause of awkward, unrhythmic movement. This anxiety, coupled with fear of an unfamiliar activity, may also result in lack of enjoyment and half-hearted participation. The beginning students should be given time to feel at ease with a new type of skill. However, if evaluation focuses on one specific, clearly defined skill, such as a traditional step pattern, a movement phrase, or a dance, it can play an important role in the identification of problem areas. Once these have been identified, more time can be spent reviewing those phases in a particular teaching progression which relate to this problem. Specific practice "prescriptions" might be given to individual students to help them achieve mastery of a particular skill. In addition to student evaluation, methods of program evaluation should also be taken into consideration.

A. Student Evaluation

Student evaluation should include evaluation of psychomotor, cognitive and affective skills.

1. Psychomotor Evaluation

Dance performance is often judged subjectively by observation. A more accurate judgment may be made if specific factors are defined and checked. Some of the factors to consider during an observation of psychomotor performance might be the following (stated in terms of the optimum performance):

a) The basic locomotor skills and/or traditional step patterns are performed accurately as far as types of weight transference are concerned.
b) The steps are performed in the correct sequence.
c) The steps and dance sequence are rhythmically accurate.
d) There is a smooth transition from one step or phrase to the next, that is, the student knows and anticipates what will come next.
e) There is a sense of dynamic phrasing, that is, the appropriate quantity and timing of energy is exerted and accents are correctly placed.
f) The rhythmic timing of the movement is correctly related to the music.
g) The spatial elements of the dance, that is, the figures executed, the size and direction of the steps and gestures, are clearly and accurately defined and coordinated with the music.
h) The total body is involved in the expression of the style and feeling of the dance.

Sample checklists follow for psychomotor evaluation of:

1. One traditional locomotor step pattern
2. A dance

1.

Name of Student_____

　　　　Traditional Locomotor Step:_____

1) Is the locomotor weight-transference pattern accurate?　　　　yes____　no____

2) Is the rhythmic pattern of the step accurate?　　　　yes____　no____

3) Are the steps coordinated with the musical timing?　　　　yes____　no____

4) Are the steps
　　too large?_____
　　too small?_____
　　correctly sized?_____

5) Is the energy expenditure　　too great?_____
　　　　　　　　　　　　　　too little?_____
　　　　　　　　　　　　　　appropriate?_____

　　Are the dynamic accents correctly placed?　　yes____　no____

6) Is the body carriage　　good　　fair　　poor____

2.

Name of Student_____

　　　　Dance:_____

1) Is the step pattern sequence correct?　　　　yes____　no____

2) Are there smooth transitions from one pattern or figure to the next?　　yes____　no____

3) Is there expression of the style and feeling of the dance?　　yes____　no____

A series of psychomotor skill tests could also be developed to determine if specific skill objectives have been achieved within each lesson. For example, in Sample Lesson Plan Two *(Fjaskern),* the skill outcome would be to walk accurately to the basic beat of the music. (A moderate tempo from the middle of the record should be played since accuracy of timing during the fast part of the record should not be expected at a beginning level). A more challenging skill resulting from this same lesson would be to walk accurately (with the music) a phrase of sixteen walking steps in one direction, turning (without pausing on the sixteenth step), to walk sixteen steps in the opposite direction. These testing procedures could be accomplished by:

    a) An on-going self-evaluation check list.
    b) Fellow student evaluation in couples or groups of four, using cards to be signed and handed in.
    c) Checking by the instructor.

Name tags or numbers may help to speed up the evaluation procedure. If the evaluation is based on the student's performance of an entire dance pattern, time for review and practice should be allowed beforehand.

2. Cognitive Evaluation

In addition to the evaluation of the performance or physical skills of each student, give a written examination. A theoretical understanding of dance terminology, the dance steps learned and the rhythmic concepts presented, may sometimes help to clarify and aid in the motor learning process. It may also help the student gain a sense of accomplishment and mastery of an area of knowledge independent of motor skills and coordination abilities. If the dance has been presented within the context of history, social studies, or geography instruction, it may be more relevant to the student. A short written quiz, or a more extensive objective knowledge test can be given examining areas of knowledge such as: the country or ethnic areas of origin for a particular dance, the translation of the dance title if it is a foreign word or phrase, the role the dance played in its cultural community, and so on.

3. Affective Evaluation

The main objective in teaching folk dance as a Physical Education activity should be to present an enjoyable, vigorous movement activity with opportunities for social inter-relationships. For most students, folk dance will not lead to competition or professional performance. While a highly-skilled dancer can gain not only a sense of achievement but social approbation from fellow students, less gifted students can also gain enjoyment and greater physical well-being. The affective contributions of enthusiasm, leadership and considerate, helpful relationships with partners and group members can add enormously to the enjoyment of all participants and should be taken into consideration as an important part of any student evaluation.

B. Program Evaluation

The particular dances selected and the pace of the progression should be evaluated continually in light of student interest, capability and progress. Student interest in folk dance activity might be gauged by providing records and record players or tapes and cassette recorders for a short period of individual or couple practice and review before, after, or outside of class. This interest can be maintained and encouraged by extracurricular noon-hour dancing, a folk dance club, performances, and ethnic parties or festivals. Program evaluation questionnaires may also be used to assess the program, teaching and facilities.

C. Conclusion

In any form of evaluation it should be recognized that competence in individual basic skills, as well as the acquisition of vocabulary and theoretical understanding, will gradually be developed over a considerable length of time. Perfection in any single skill should not be required of the students before they progress to more challenging skills, particularly since the fundamentals will be reviewed constantly and put to use even in learning more complex steps and dances. It should be remembered that even a simple dance requires the *coordination* of many skills. It takes time before all these kaleidoscopic fragments of isolated skills fall into position so that a total dance pattern can be performed effortlessly and enjoyably. The goal of enthusiastic enjoyment and, hopefully, an interest in further and possibly even lifelong participation should be kept in mind, and students given encouragement and confidence in their abilities at every stage of their progress.

Chapter Six
Dance Descriptions

A. Introduction

This chapter contains dance descriptions for the Level I dances described in the Sample Lesson Plan Progression presented in Chapter Three. While space limitations prevented a detailed lesson plan presentation of Level II and III material, dance descriptions have also been included for a sample progression of nine Level II dances and skills, as well as several Level III dances which can be used to teach turning skills. Dance descriptions have *not* been included for all the dances listed in the Activity Sequence Chart.

The dance descriptions are presented in the accepted format used by the Folk Dance Federation of California. Abbreviations used are explained in the List of Abbreviations, (see page 13).

These descriptions are as detailed as possible. However, it is preferable to learn a dance from a qualified instructor, using the description only as a memory aid. *Strange permutations may occur when an unfamiliar dance is worked up from a written description.* In most cases, the pattern of each dance described is a standardized, generally-accepted version. If this version is taught accurately, students will be able to participate in future folk dance enjoyment wherever they may encounter folk dance groups. If they have learned a different version, confusion and arguments may occur. As well, words are inadequate to describe the subtleties of styling — an important part of the ethnic flavor of each dance. This is best learned from an ethnic specialist.

B. Index of Dance Descriptions

Level I - A sample progresson of dances presenting basic locomotor and rhythmic skills.

1. Pata Pata
2. Fjäskern
3. Troika
4. D'Hammerschmiedsgselln
5. The Crested Hen
6. Gigue Aux Six
7. La Raspa
8. Pljeskavac Kolo

Level II - A sample progression of more complex dances introducing sideways crossing steps (1-4) and traditional locomotor step patterns in their basic form (5-9).

1. Ersko Kolo
2. Fast Hasapikos
3. Armenian Misirlou
4. Cherkessiya
5. Schottische For Fours
6. Cotton-Eyed Joe 'Kicker' Dance
7. Polka Zu Dreien
8. The Dashing White Sergeant
9. Norwegian Mountain March

Level III - Several dances at a higher skill level which use traditional locomotor step patterns in their turning form

1. Free-Style Couple Schottische
2. Doudlebska Polka
3. Bitte Mand I Knibe (Little Man In A Fix)

C. Level I Dances

1. Pata Pata (South Africa)

Pata Pata (PAH-ta PAH-ta) is probably a composed dance based on African-type movements. There are many variations in styling and basic pattern, and body, hand, and arm movements are very improvisational.

Music: Reprise 0732, recorded by Miriam Makeba

Formation: Individuals scattered throughout the dance space, facing the music or instructor to begin the first pattern. The dance pattern is repeated each time with the dancers facing a different direction, since the last phrase includes a 1/4 turn CW.

Steps: Touch-step, walk, heel-toe swivel

Meter: 4/4   Dance Pattern

Measures

1-2   Introduction (8 cts.)

1   Touch R toe diag. fwd. R (ct. 1). Step R beside L (ct. 2). Repeat cts. 1-2 using L ft. (cts. 3, 4).

2   Starting with ft. parallel and close together, knees loose, shift wt. forward to balls of ft. and move both heels apart (ct. 1); shift wt. to heels and move toes apart (ct. 2); shift wt. to toes and move heels together (ct. 3); shift wt. to heels and move toes together (ct. 4). (cts. 1-4 equals heels, toes, heels, **toes**).

3   Bring R knee across in front of L leg, rotating R leg in and bending knee (ct. 1); touch R toe to R side (ct. 2), bring R knee across in front

4   of L knee again (ct. 3); step on R beside L (ct. 4).

4   Pivoting on ball of R ft., make 1/4 turn R or CW, and kick straight L leg forward, clapping at the same time (ct. 1); back up with 3 walking steps L (ct. 2); R (ct. 3); L (ct. 4).

Repeat dance from beginning facing new direction.

Note: Meas. 2 is a challenging coordination. Two easier variations are: a) Keep wt. on balls of ft. and open heels apart (ct. 1); close heels together (ct. 2); repeat heels apart and together (cts. 3, 4), or b) keep feet parallel and move sideward to R, swiveling first with heels leading, then toes, (cts. 1, 2); repeat (cts. 3, 4). Whatever pattern is used it must take a total of 4 counts or 1 meas. of the music.

2. Fjäskern (Sweden)

Fjaskern (FYESS-kehrn) is a folk dance circle mixer from southern Sweden, simple enough for the first number at an initial session of beginners, yet exciting enough to provide hilarious fun for even the most calloused old timers. Secret: the music accelerates from almost ridiculously slow to nearly (but not quite) impossibly fast. Hence the dance's English title: "Hurry-Scurry."

Source: As learned in Sweden in 1950 by Gordon E. Tracie and taught at Skandia Folkdance Society, Seattle.

Music: Viking V-200 (obtainable from Viking Record Sales, 1612 N. 53rd St., Seattle, Washington, 98103, U.S.A.)

Formation: Couples in double circle, M on inside, W on outside, Beg. facing LOD. Open position, inside hands, when joined, at shoulder level; free hands on hips Swedish style (fingers fwd, thumb back).

Steps: Walking, running, kicking steps. Footwork is parallel (same for M and W). Throughout the entire dance there is a simple L-R alternation of the ft., without stop.

Styling: Sprightly and with humor.

Meter: 4/4   Dance Pattern

Measures

A. Circle Fwd and Back

1-4   Inside hands joined, beg. on L ft., cpls move fwd in LOD 16 steps.*

1-4   Turning around individually, twd ptr, other hands are joined, and cpls move back in opp. direction in similar manner with 16 steps, again beg. on L ft.

B. Kick and Exchange Places

5   Facing ptr squarely, M on inside, W on outside of circle, both hands on own hips, cpls dance 4 kicking steps, *beg. with wt. on L ft* (kicking R ft. fwd).

6   With handclap on 1st beat, ptrs change places with 4 running steps, moving about CW while facing each other (as if hands were joined).

7-8   Repeat the action of meas. 5-6 to return to own place.

5-8   Repeat the action of meas. 5-8 above. Repeat entire dance from the beginning. *Ptr change* is effected as sequence begins with A. Simplest way is for M to move fwd to next W, inasmuch as being on inside of circle, M has shorter distance to go.

Note: For the 1st two sequences of A, walking steps are used; succeeding sequences are running steps.
Presented by Gordon E. Tracie, Stockton Folk Dance Camp, 1962. Dance description revised and included by permission of Gordon E. Tracie.

3. Troika (Russia)

Troika (TROY-ka) means a threesome, and refers to the three horses which were used to pull the sleighs or carriages of the Russian noble families.

Source: This is the original form of the dance as it was introduced by Michael and Mary Ann Herman in the U.S.A. many years ago.

Music: Folk Dancer MH or CMH 1059, Folkraft 1170.

Formation: Lines of three dancers, either a man and two women, one woman and two men, or all men or all women, arranged in wheelspoke formation, all facing counterclockwise. The three people stand side by side, joining their inside hands, right foot free, free arms held out at the sides somewhat.

Steps: Run, stamp.

Meter: 4/8   Dance Pattern

Measures

1-2   Introduction

A. Running Fwd.

1-4   All run forward for 16 steps starting R, lifting knees. Be careful not to make this a goose-kick step with straight legs. Dancers should take light running steps, just skimming the floor as they swiftly flow over it.

B. Arches

5-6 Center dancer raises hand joined with left-hand dancer to form an arch. Right-hand dancer runs under arch, circling CCW with 8 steps. (Center person must also turn under his own left hand following the one going under otherwise figure won't work.) Left-hand dancer runs in place. Keep inside hands joined but with a loose handhold.

7-8 Center dancer raises hand joined to right-hand dancer to form an arch, and left-hand dancer runs 8 steps in a CW circle under arch and back to place, center dancer also turning under again. Right-hand dancer runs in place.

C. Circle

9-11 Left-hand dancer continues running CW toward right-hand dancer, joining hands to form a circle of three. All run lightly in a circle to the left (CW) with 12 running steps.

12 Stamp Right, Left, Right, (hold), turning to face to the right.

13-16 Repeat action of meas. 9-12, running lightly to the right (CCW) for 12 steps and stamping three stamps. If not done as a mixer, the two outside people drop joined hands and re-form the line of 3 facing LOD on the last 3 stamps, ready to repeat the dance from the beginning. To make dance progressive, the two outside people raise their joined hands to form an arch and the center person moves forward under the arch to the center position in the set of dancers ahead of him, joining hands with the two new outside people. As soon as the center person has passed under the arch, the two outside people drop their joined hands and stand, facing forward, leaving a space between them for the new center person. The pass-under occurs during the last measure (16).

Dance description included by permission of Michael Herman.

4. D'Hammerschmiedsgselln (Bavaria, Germany)

D'Hammerschmiedsgselln (Duh-HAHM-mer-shmeetz-guh-zehl-en) which means the journeyman blacksmith, was originally a dance for four men with a chorus using a clap and slap pattern in a mock-fighting action, interspersed with different figures. It was introduced as a men's dance at Stockton (California) Folk Dance Camp in 1964 by Huig Hofman of Belgium. A two-couple version, adapted for recreational dancing, is described in the dance description which accompanies the record, written by Rickey Holden. This version is the one described below.

Music: Folkraft 1485 (45 rpm), or Folkraft LP-5.

Formation: Circle of 4 people, either 4 men:

or 2 couples:
Woman #1 facing woman #2,
Man #1 facing man #2.

Steps: Uneven step-hop, or slow skip in waltztime; step (cts. 1,2), hop (ct. 3); 1/2 turn waltz (optional).

Meter: 3/4   Dance Pattern

Measures

1-4 Introduction

1-16 Chorus: Slap and Clap Pattern (Music A)

1 Slap own thighs, bending knees slightly (ct.1); slap own waist (or men, chest) (ct.2); clap own hands together (ct.3).

2 Clap opposite person's R hand with own R (ct.1); clap opposite person's L hand with own L (ct.2); clap both hands with opposite's two hands (ct. 3).

Note: One pair starts on meas. 1 (men #1 + 3) the other pair starts the same pattern one measure later. If two-couple version is done, designate whether men or women start on meas. 1 (it is done both ways). In either case, one pair is doing the cross-over claps while the other is doing the slaps and claps with their own bodies. The second pair to start will only do half of the last pattern.

1-16 Figure I: Circles

1-8 All join hands in a circle and do 8 slow waltz skips or uneven step-hops circling left (CW).

9-16 Circle R with 8 skips (CCW).

1-16 Figure II: Stars

1-8 Join 4 hands in a RH star (sometimes done in a "fireman's carry" wrist-hold) and do 8 waltz skips CW turning the star.

9-16 Turn inward toward the center, dropping hands, put 4 hands in to form a LH star and turn it CCW with 8 waltz skips.

1-16 Figure III: Large Circle or Couple Waltz

1-8 All groups in the room join in one large circle and waltz skip 8 skips to the L (CW).

9-16 All circle R with 8 skips.

Optional Figure III or end pattern: Individual couples (man with women on his right), take ballroom hold and do a turning waltz (1/2 turns CW) anywhere in the room.

Dance Pattern: Chorus, Figure I, Chorus, Figure II, Chorus, Figure III. Entire sequence is done only once through.

Note: The men, particularly, can add to the fun of the dance by miming a very strong, aggressive slap to the opposite man, with a preparatory lean back and body thrust forward, as long as they " pull their punch" at the last second. The women can do the claps more daintily.

5. Den Toppede Høne (The Crested Hen) (Denmark)

Den Toppede Høne means "The Crested Hen," referring to the fact that in Denmark the men wore red stocking caps with a tassel representing a rooster comb. The ladies added to the fun of the dance by trying to pull the man's cap off as he went through the arch. If successful, then the lady became "crested" hen.

Music: Record: Folkraft 1159, 1194; RCA LMP 1624; EPA 4143; Tanz 58 402; World of Fun LP 4. Piano: Burchenal, Elizabeth, *Folk Dances of Denmark,* p. 49. LaSalle, Dorothy, *Rhythms and Dances for Elementary Schools,* p. 150. N.P. Neilson, and Van Hagen, W., *Physical Education for Elementary Schools,* p. 300.

Formation: Set of three, two ladies and a man, hands joined to form a circle.

Step: Step-hop.

Meter 2/4	Dance Pattern

Measures

Part I

1-8 Beginning left, step-hop around circle clockwise, taking a vigorous stamp on first beat. Dancers lean away from center as they circle.

1-8 Jump, bringing feet down sharply on first beat, step-hop around circle counterclockwise.

Part II

9-10 Continuing step-hop, ladies release joined hands, place free hand on hip, and right-hand lady dances through arch made by man and left-hand lady.

11-12 Man turns under his left arm, following right-hand lady through arch.

13-14 Left-hand lady dances through arch made by man and right-hand lady.

15-16 Man turns under his right arm, following left-hand lady through arch.

9-16 Repeat action of measures 9-16.

Mixer: The man may progress forward to the next group at the completion of part II.

Above dance description is reproduced as presented in the Fifth Edition (1978) of **Dance A While** *p.234 by permission of Jane Harris, Anne Pittman, and Marlys Waller.*

6. Gigue Aux Six (Val Morin, Quebec, Canada)

Gigue aux Six (ZHEEG O SEECE) is a French Canadian dance for three couples in longways formation, which was collected by Dale Hyde and included in his album *Folk Dances of French Canada.*

Music: *Folk Dances of French Canada for Canadian Children,* Dancecraft LP 123321, band 3, Reel à Gaston, or band 6, Reel de Campbellton, or any French Canadian reel music (in 2/4 or 4/4), which is an *evenly-phrased* 32 bar structure.

Formation: Longways set for 3 cpls. (a line of 3 men facing a line of 3 women), head or active cpl. closest to the music, men with L shoulders toward the music.

Steps: Balance or step-swing, buzz-step couple swing, walk, side slide.

Meter: 4/4	Dance Pattern

Measures

A. Head cpl. balance, swing and cast-off.

1 Head cpl. balance to the R, facing each other; Step R (ct. 1), swing L leg low across in front of R (ct.2); then balance to the left; as in cts. 1 and 2 with opposite ftwk. (cts. 3, 4).

2 Head cpl. does partner swing using modified shoulder-waist position (man puts back of both thumbs just under woman's shoulder blades, rest of hand hanging down loosely), and turns once using 4 buzz-steps; (step R ct. 1, step side L, ct. *and*). In French Canadian swing, partners face each other squarely and keep the inside borders of their R feet beside each other. They alternate stepping down on the R foot, (ct. 1), with a sideways step onto the left foot (ct. *and*). A pulling action rotates the body around as the R ft. pivots, heel slightly off the floor. A walk-around swing or a Western Square Dance buzz swing in hip-to-hip position, may be easier for beginners unaccustomed to French Canadian styling.

3-4 Head cpl. separates, (M turns L, W turns R), and each casts off, walking down behind his or her own line to meet at the bottom of the set (total of 8 cts.). Other 2 cpls. remain in place.

B. Head couple (now in 3rd position), balance, swing and slide up and back.

5-6   Head cpl. repeat the balance and swing as in meas. 1-2, Figure A above.

7-8   Joining both hands, head cpl. does 4 side slides, (or 3 1/2 plus a hop) up the center of the set toward the top; then 4 side slides back down the center of the set to third position. Dance repeats from the beginning with original second couple now the active couple in first place, and continues with the third cpl. as heads, etc. until the end of the music.

Note: The dance pattern as described above is adapted from the dance description written by Dale Hyde for the booklet which accompanies the record. It is also possible to add to the challenge of this dance or most other French Canadian set dances by having people learn and perform a few simple gigue steps which can be done at will by the inactive people while standing in place. The gigue was originally a solo form of dance, often competitive, but in more recent times it is also done as an optional embellishment in set dances. To do gigue steps well, particularly up to tempo, takes considerable practice and requires hard-soled shoes (often modern taps are used in addition). However, trying a few steps can be fun for even a beginner if accuracy and clarity of sound production are not emphasized too strongly, and a shuffle-type of step is used.

Practice exercises:

a) Stand with weight on L, and let R leg hang loosely, R foot just clearing the floor, slightly more forward than L foot. Sharply tap the ball of the R ft. on the floor, lifting foot up quickly, moving only in the ankle joint. Do this several times with the R ft., then put wt. on the R and try this with the L.

b) Tap the R foot as above, using the sharp ankle action, but straighten the knee so that the leg is straight and stretched slightly forward, then tap the R ft. again, slightly bending the knee. The forward-back action is very small and the foot always remains close to the floor. Start slowly and gradually increase speed. Practice with both legs.

Gigue Step #1 (1 meas. pattern done in reel-time 2/4 meter)

Measures

1   With wt. on L, tap ball of R ft. straightening knee as in practice exercise above, and straightening supporting leg as well (ct. 1); tap ball of same ft. again, bending R knee slightly (ct. *and*) as above; step R, putting wt. on whole ft., bending supporting leg slightly (ct. 2).

2   As in meas. 1 but with opp. ftwk.

Gigue Step #2 (2 meas. pattern done to reel-time 2/4 meter)

1   Wt. on L, do gigue step #1 with R ft. tapping, as in meas. 1 above. (tap, tap, step).

2   Step up onto ball of L ft. straightening knee (ct. 1), step down to whole R ft, bending knee slightly (ct. 2).

3-4   Do pattern as in meas. 1 and 2 above, but with opp. ftwk.

Note: While doing gigue steps, body remains erect and arms usually hang loosely at sides.

Dance included by permission of Dale Hyde

7. La Raspa (Mexico-U.S.A.)

According to Michael and Mary Ann Herman, La Raspa is thought to be an American novelty dance using Mexican music rather than a Mexican dance. It is sometimes called the Mexican Hat Dance although there is a traditional dance, Jarabe Tapatio, using a man's sombrero and many intricate heel and toe-tapping steps which is more properly referred to by that name. Other popular names for La Raspa (which means the rasp, a Mexican instrument) include the Shuffle Dance, the Scissors Dance, and the File. The first step pattern is known as the Bleking jump in Swedish folk dance and is also found in the Danish "Ace of Diamonds," Lithuanian "Noriu Miego," German "Herr Schmidt" and in the Serbian "Kolenike."

Music: RCA EPA-4139 *La Raspa and other folk dances* (45 rpm), RCA LPM 1623 *All-Purpose Folk Dances,* Folkraft 1457 (45 rpm).

Formation: Varied. May be done in couple scatter formation, partners facing each other with both hands joined, or not holding hands, man holding his clasped hands behind his back, woman holding skirt, or may be done in a circle of cpls. or without partners, all facing the center.

Steps: Bleking jump, running steps or fast skipping.

Meter: 2/4   Dance Pattern

Measures   *Note:* There is no one set sequence but rather, many variations which can be adapted to the group situation and levels as long as the constants (the Bleking jump in Pt. I and the running or skipping in Pt. II) are maintained.

4   Introduction

Part I: 8 Bleking jump patterns (16 meas.)

1-2 Beginning with wt. on R, take one Bleking jump: Jump onto L ft. in place, placing R ft. forward on floor, heel down, toe up at the same time. The take-off into the jump is on the up-beat of the measure before, the landing on ct. 1 ("uh-one"). Jump onto R ft. in place, changing the placement of the two ft. so that the L ft. moves back. (ct. "uh-two"). Jump a third time, changing back to original placement of ft. (meas. 2, ct. "uh-one"). Pause, holding position, (meas. 2, ct.2).

3-4 Repeat above Bleking jump pattern but with opp. ftwk.

5-16 Repeat Bleking jumps 6 more times, alternating ftwk.

Note: Bleking jumps can be done facing ptr. or center of circle, or if in cpls., once facing, once facing opp. directions, R shoulder to R shoulder, once facing, once facing opp. directions, L. shoulder to L shoulder (and repeat). If in a circle or line of men only, the Bleking jump may be done in a more physically challenging way by gradually going further into a deep knee squat position with each jump pattern.

Part II: Any of several traveling figures, using a run or fast skipping step. (16 meas.) 2 runs or skips per meas.)

Variation I

Clap own hands once, then hook right elbows with ptr., skip or run around for 8 steps (CW). Clap hands again, hook left elbows and run or skip around 8 steps (CCW). Repeat R and L elbow turns.

Variation II

Use 16 steps for 2 R elbow turns, 16 steps for 2 L elbow turns. No repeat.

Variation III

As a mixer: From a single circle of cpls. do a "Grand Right and Left" running for 32 steps, W-CW, M-CCW. Start with ptrs. facing, R hands joined. Repeat dance with new ptr. each time.

Variation IV

No ptrs, all standing in single circle, facing center hands joined. Bleking jumps can be done, alternately facing slightly R and L, Part II running or skipping 16 steps CW and 16 steps CCW.

Note: The number of measures in Pts. I and II is described according to the version recorded for RCA by Michael Herman's Folk Dance Orchestra. Other recordings may vary.

8. Pljeskavac Kolo (Serbia, Yugoslavia)

There are many different kolo (originally meaning circle or wheel) dance patterns which are popular in Serbia and other parts of Yugoslavia, as well as Serbian-American ethnic communities; they can play an important role in folk dance programing since most do not require partners or a set number of participants. According to Miriam Lidster, Pljeskavac (PLEHS-kah-vahtz or PLYES-KAH-vahtz) was learned from a Romanian by members of the Banat Tamburitza Orchestra who recorded a number of Serbian dances for the Herman's Folk Dancer label. They put this dance to a Serbian melody and taught it to the Hermans. Since then, it has become one of the most popular kolos in the International Folk Dance repertory. Although the first step pattern is a common one found in the dances of many Balkan countries, as well as in other Serbian dances such as Haj, Haj Boze Daj and Radikalko, it is listed in some books as Romanian-American because of its origin. The title means Clap Dance and the stamping and clapping pattern makes it especially lively and enjoyable for beginners. Occasional spontaneous shouts of "Hopa," "Hey," or a high, shrill "eeya" express and generate enjoyment and enthusiasm.

Music: Folk Dancer MH 1009, Folkraft 1548, Festival 4817.

Formation: Broken circle, leader at the R end, hands joined in "V" position, straight down, dancers almost shoulder to shoulder, bodies erect and proud. End people may have free hand on hips, fingers fwd.; hand in loosely-clenched fist behind the back; or thumb tucked into vest armhole.

Steps: Small, bouncy walk, even step-hop, stamp (taking wt.).

Meter: 2/4   Dance Pattern

Measures

A. Walking in zig-zag patterns

1 Facing and walking diagonally R, (circle moves CCW and inward), walk R, L, (cts. 1, 2).

2 Three small walking steps, R, L, R, (cts. 1 *and* 2), either continuing in a diagonal R direction or in place, facing the center.

3 Facing the center, walk backward two steps, L, R, (circle expands), (cts. 1, 2).

4 In place or moving further backward, three small steps, L, R, L (cts. 1 *and* 2).

5-8 Repeat above pattern meas. 1-4.

B. To center and back with stamps and claps

1 Walk toward center two steps, R, L, (cts. 1, 2).

2	Keeping hands joined, stamp 3 times alternating feet; R, L, R, (cts. 1 and 2).
3	Back away from center with two steps, L, R, (cts. 1, 2)
4	Step 3 steps in place, L, R, L (cts. 1 and 2) and simultaneously clap own hands together 3 times.
5-8	Repeat meas. 1-4, Fig. II.

Note: The above walking version is in the musical rhythm of: S, S, Q, Q, S. The leader can wind the line in any direction he or she chooses and may change to the following, more vigorous and challenging version of Figure I after the dancers have "warmed-up." This step can be continued until the end of the music, or the leader may alternate the walking and step-hop versions. The leader may signal the change from one to the other by shouting "hopa" or waving a hand or handkerchief.

Measures

A. Step-hops plus walks (or schottische step) in zig-zags

1	2 even step-hops, R, R, L, L, traveling diagonally R (cts. 1 and 2 and)
2	As in meas. 2, Fig. I above, or 3 walking or running steps plus a hop; R, L, R, R, which is a schottische step (cts. 1 and 2 and) traveling diag. R.
3	Backing away from the center, 2 even step-hops; L, L, R, R, (cts. 1 and 2 and)
4	As in meas. 4 above, Fig. 1, or 3 steps and 1 hop in place or continuing to travel backward with small steps; L, R, L, L, (cts. 1 and 2 and).
5-8	Repeat above pattern, meas. 1-4.

B. Remains the same as Walking version, Part II above--the steps are slow, walking ones.

Note: In dancing the vigorous version of Fig. A, uncomfortable pulling and "cracking the whip" can be avoided if the individual steps remain small and arms are not allowed to stretch wide apart. Inevitably, most people at some time will forget, and clap when they should be stamping or vice versa--this is part of the fun of the dance and should not be cause for embarrassment.

D. Level II Dances

1. Ersko Kolo (Serbia, Yugoslavia)

The dance Ersko kolo (air'-sko ko'-lo) was formerly popular at weddings, fairs and other village social events in and around the town of Užice (oo'-zhee-tseh) in the republic of Serbia, Yugoslavia.

The word *ersko* is derived from *ero* (air' -oh), a nickname applied by other Serbians to people from the Užice area. *Ersko kolo* thus means "dance done by the villagers around Užice." It is the name by which the dance is known among folk dance groups and Physical Education teachers in other parts of Yugoslavia and in North America. Around Užice itself, Ersko kolo was called by a number of different names: Šesnaestica (shess'-nigh-stee-tsah, "sixteen-count dance"), Ja idok (yah ee'-doke), Ja brdom (yah brr'-dome) (these last two names taken from lines of the song sometimes sung to the dance's melody).

Music: Folk Dancer MH 3020-A, *Ersko kolo;* Folkraft F-1498 45rpm, Ersko kolo.

Formation: Open circle or curved line, hands joined at sides in "V" position. End dancers place free hand at small of back.

Meter: 4/4	Dance Pattern

Measures

Part I - Slow

1	Facing center, step R ft sideways R, weight on heel (ct. 1); step L ft behind R ft (ct. and); step R ft sideways R as above (ct. 2); again step L ft behind R ft (ct and).
2-7	Repeat action of meas. 1, moving continually R.
8	Stamp R ft in place (ct. 1); stamp L ft (no weight) in place (ct. 2).
9-16	Repeat movements of meas. 1-8 with opposite footwork and direction (beginning L ft and moving sideways L, etc.). End with weight on L ft, R ft raised slightly.

Part II - Fast

17-18	Turning 1/4 R to face directly CCW, run 3 steps, starting R ft (ct. 1), L ft (ct. 2), R ft (ct. 1, meas. 2), hop R ft (ct. 2), moving CCW. (The 3 runs and hop are similar to a schottische step).
19-20	Without turning around, run bkwd (moving clockwise): L, R, L, hop, turning on hop to face center.
21-22	Moving toward center, run fwd 3 steps and hop: R, L, R, hop.
23-24	Moving out from center, run bkwd 3 steps and hop: L,R,L, hop.
25-32	Repeat movements of meas. 17-24

Repeat dance from the beginning.

Notes and description by Dick Crum. Dance description included by permission of Dick Crum.

2. Hasapikos (Fast) (Greece)

Hasapikos (Hah-SAH-peeh-kos) was originally a Byzantine dance of the Butchers' Guild and possibly has even more ancient origins. It is now done in many versions throughout various parts of Greece. In fact, the basic step pattern is one of the most universally popular ones, found all over the Balkans and Middle East. It is known among folk dancers as the "fast" Hasapikos to distinguish it from the Varys or "slow, heavy" hasapikos of *Never On Sunday* fame, and the Hasaposervikos, a moderately slow dance. There are many variations on the basic step, a few of which are listed below, and it is up to the leader to decide which will be done, in what order, and for how long. The leader can progress from one to the other at will, or intersperse the basic step with different variations.

Music: Folkraft LP-8, Folkraft F1021.

Formation: Lines, leader on right end, "T" position or "W" position. R foot free.

Step: Walk, step-swing, heel-toe swivel, jump, side slide.

Meter 2/4	Dance Pattern

Measures

Introduction: Leader may start at any time since the 3 meas. basic pattern will tend to overlap the musical phrasing.

A. Basic Step

1   Step sideways R on R ft. (ct. 1), cross and step on L ft *behind* R (ct. 2).
       Note: Ct. 2 is also done stepping in *front* of R.

2-3   Step R (ct. 1), swing L ft across in front (ct. 2) Step L in place, (ct. 1) swing R ft across in front (ct. 2).

B. Some Variations (in random order)

i "Lean"

1   Tip trunk of body forward slightly at hip joint, back straight, as step side R (ct. 1). L leg arcs around behind R leg before step L in back of R (ct. 2).

2-3   As in basic step

ii "Swivels"

1-?   Progressing sideways LOD, move heels to R (ct. 1), put weight on them, move toes to R (ft parallel) (ct. 2) put weight on them. Continue as long as leader wishes.

iii "Basic with Pas de Basque"

1   As above basic meas. 1

2   Leap to R with R ft (ct. 1). Step on L crossing over in front of R (ct. *and*). Step on R in place (ct. 2).

3   Repeat meas. 2 (Pas de Basque) with opp. ftwk.

iv "Turn"

1   Releasing hands, two walking steps R, L, turning once around CW.

2   As in basic.
       Note: This is done by the leader only, traditionally, but can be done recreationally with first the leader turning alone, then the leader plus second person, then the leader plus persons two and three, and so on. This is more effective when lines are short. Another turning variation is to have the leader turn first alone, then everyone turn until the leader signals a change.

v "Jumps"

1   Jump into side stride position, feet apart (ct. 1)
       Jump into closed ft position, R ft crossed in front of Left, (feet comfortably turned out, R heel to L toe) (ct. 2)

2   As in meas. 1, ct. 1 above, (ct. 1)
       Jump into closed ft position, *L* ft in front (ct. 2)
       or

1   Alternate crossing right ft in front and crossing L, without the jump apart (cts. 1, 2).

2-3   Repeat meas. 1 above

vi "Slides"

1   As a traveling step in order to move the line to another place in the room or to cut through another line if they are doing the men's swivel (see below), one can travel sideways R with a side slide; step side R with R ft., (ct. 1), close L to R, leaping on it, (ct. "uh")

vii "Combined Basic and Slides"

1   Two slides sideways R (cts. "one-uh-two-uh")
2-3   As in **basic:** two step swings.

viii "Men's Swivels"

1   As in plain swivels (see variation ii above) but men, if in separate line, gradually bend knees into squatting position as they swivel, and can break out of shoulder hold and turn individually in squat position in a clockwise circle in place.

Notes by Marcia Snider. Adapted from notes by Athan Karras, Reed College Folk Dance Camp, 1961, and notes from **Greek Folk Dances** *by Rickey Holden and Mary Vouras.*

3. Armenian Misirlou (Armenia)

This version of Misirlou should not be confused with the Greek-American Kritikos-type pattern also done to the same music. This step pattern was a popular one among the Armenian Americans living in Fresno, California, and was used in several of their dances. It was possibly put to this music by Frances Ajoian, the leader of their dance group for many years. It was introduced at Stockton Folk Dance Camp by John Filcich in 1961 and has become very popular in many international folk dance groups. More recently, Tom Bozigian has taught the dance using an Armenian piece of music called Sirdes (Express 33 1/3 A-101B) which is used by Armenian youth organizations in Los Angeles.

Music: Festival 3505-A (45 rpm) *Misirlou*

Formation: Open circle, leader at R end, hands held in a close W hold, with little fingers linked and hands held near one's own shoulders. If the little fingers are loosely held in a "cuphook" shape and the dancers remain close together—almost shoulder to shoulder—this position is a much more comfortable one. Line can be spiraled or wound in different directions.

Step: Walk, touch.

Styling: This dance should be done with a flowing quality of movement--steps are fairly small and the knees are flexible.

Meter 2/4   Dance Pattern

Measures

4   Introduction
1   Facing center, weight on R ft, point L across in front of R ft (cts. 1, 2)
2   Keeping weight on R, point L to L side about 12 inches (cts. 1, 2)
3-4   Repeat actions of meas. 1 *and* 2 above.
5   Step L across in front of R, taking weight on L (cts. 1, 2)
6   Swinging R leg around, step R across in front of L, taking weight (cts. 1, 2)
7   Step L across in front of R (ct. 1), step R to R side (ct. 2).
8   Step L crossing behind R (ct. 1), step R to R side (ct. 2).
       Note: Meas. 7 and 8 constitute a 4-step grapevine pattern done twice as fast as movements in meas. 1 thru 6.

       Repeat dance phrase until the end of the music.

4. Cherkassiya (Tscherkessia) (Israel)

Cherkassiya (Chair-kuh-SEE-ya) is an Israeli dance with step patterns derived from the dances of the Circassians, a minority group who immigrated to Palestine from the plains of southeastern Russia at the beginning of the nineteenth century. The movement is said to portray horses or riders. The dance consists of a chorus pattern which travels in a CW direction, interspersed with various figures or step-patterns which are done in place or move in a CCW direction. On the

Israeli Folk Dances LP no. 7, the figures are called in Hebrew and English, but the Tikva LP is an instrumental version, leaving room for a choice of figures either by the leader on the RH end of the line, or by the group. The sequence described below is the one which is called plus suggestions for alternative figures.

Music: Tikva LP 106-*Israeli Dance Medley for Children*.
          Israel Music Foundation LP-7 *Israeli Folk Dances*.

Formation: Short straight lines of 4 or 5 dancers in back basket hold or (easier for beginners) with hands joined down "V" position. Leader on the R end of the line holding a kerchief to signal changes. Wt. on L ft.

Step: Walk, run, step-hop.

Meter 2/4   Dance Pattern

Measures

1-4   Introduction (I.M.F. LP-7)
1-8   Introduction (Tikva LP-106)
       A. *Chorus* (8 measures)
1   Traveling sideways in a CW direction, accent first beat by stamping with R ft across in front of L, taking wt., bending knee slightly and leaning fwd. with body (ct. 1); step sideward L with L ft. (small step) straightening body (ct. 2)
2   Step behind L ft. with R ft. (ct. 1); step side L with L ft. (ct. 2)
3-8   Repeat 4-beat grapevine combination (meas. 1 and 2) three more times.
       B. Figures (8 meas. each)

                    i "Waves"

Facing and traveling in CCW direction, 8 step-hops, starting R, bending free leg at knee on each step and kicking it straight fwd. on hop.

                    ii "Scissors Forward"

In place, alternate leaping onto R and L, 16 times, kicking free straight leg fwd, leaning back with trunk of body.

                    iii "Step and Shuffle"

Facing forward and traveling sideways to the right, step or leap onto R leg to the R side, simultaneously brushing straight L leg to the left side (ct. 1), stepping behind R leg with L, bending both knees slightly (ct. 2) 8 step-and-shuffle steps.

                    iv "Scissors in Reverse"

As in figure ii above but lean trunk of body fwd and kick free straight leg backward, starting with leap onto R; 16 leaps.

v "Horse Trot"

Facing and moving in a CCW direction following leader, run 16 steps lifting bent knees high on each step, starting R.

vi "The Locomotive"

Facing and moving in a CCW direction, put both hands on the waist of the person in front and walk with 16 small stamping steps, knees bent, back straight.

Other Variations

Combination of 8 fwd. scissors kicks and 8 backward scissors.

8 toe-heel swivel steps to R side, facing center.

Instead of vi above, do 16 steps facing and traveling CCW, in a deep-knee squat position.

Dance Pattern alternates Chorus (8 meas.) and Figure (8 meas.).

5. Schottische for Fours (Scandinavia-U.S.A.)

Schottische for Fours, or Horse and Buggy Schottische as it is sometimes called, was taught by Olga Kulbitsky at Stockton (Calif.) Folk Dance Camp in 1957. The notes below are adapted from the Syllabus.

Music: Any schottische in moderate tempo 4/4; Folkraft 1164 or 1166 (45 rpm).

Formation: Two couples stand one behind the other, both facing LOD or CCW direction. Inside hands are joined with partner (woman stands on man's R), outside hands link the fwd. and back couples together. 2 cpl. sets can all travel in a CCW circular direction or in any direction the front cpl. wishes. The front cpl. is #1, the back cpl. is #2.

Step: schottische (step, step, step, hop), step-hop (even).

Meter 4/4   Dance Pattern

Measures

1-2	Starting with outside ft. (M-L, W-R) all travel forward with two basic schottische steps; step-close-step-hop, or run-run-run-hop, even timing.
3-4	Taking four even step-hops, cpl. #1 releases inside hands and, turning away from each other, man to the left, woman to the right, move around cpl. #2 on the outside and come together behind them, joining inside hands again. They thus become #2 cpl. and the

former #2 cpl. is now #1 cpl.

5-6	Repeat two schottische steps forward as in meas. 1-2.
7-8	Repeat 4 step-hops with new cpl #1 turning back on the outside as the old cpl. #1 did in meas. 3-4 above.
9-10	Repeat two basic schottische steps forward as in meas. 1-2.
11-12	Cpl. #1 (front cpl.) backs under raised inside hands of cpl. #2 with 4 step-hops (all hands remain joined). This action will cause cpl. #2 to "wring the dishrag" turning under their own joined hands in order to straighten themselves out. After turning,#2 cpl. has become #1 cpl.
13-14	Repeat two basic schottische steps forward.
15-16	Repeat the four step-hops, new #1 cpl. backing under joined hands as in meas. 11-12 above.

Note: This is a dance which has many versions. If there is an extra couple, the dance can be done as a couple mixer with the two couples unhitching themselves and moving toward a new couple at an indicated time. Additional two-couple figures such as LH or RH star, circle (L or R), a line with the 4 people side by side, and so on can be added, spontaneously or with pre-planning on the part of each foursome. No matter what figures are used, however, the footwork always consists of the basic schottische dance pattern; two schottische steps plus 4 step-hops.

6. Cotton-Eyed Joe 'Kicker' Dance (Texas, U.S.A.)

This dance was taught by Jimmy Brown of San Antonio, Texas at a workshop in Vancouver, October, 1974. A "kicker" is Texan slang for a cowboy. There are also other round dance patterns to the same music. Other popular dances in wheelspoke formation are Jessie Polka and Ten Pretty Girls.

Music: Folkraft 1470x45B (45 rpm).

Formation: Any number of people in a line, arms around waists, elbows linked, back basket hold or forearms clasped. Free hands, thumbs in jeans pocket. Four or five to a line is usually a manageable number. Lines are arranged in a circle like wheel spokes, all facing CCW direction.

Step: Walk, two-step.

Meter 2/4   Dance Pattern

Measures

	A. "Kicker" pattern--toward and away from center
1	With wt. on L, kick twice with free R leg, bending knee and straightening leg, pushing R heel fwd. and down toward floor (toes up as if in cowboy boots and stirrups) leaning back with upper body, (cts. 1, 2).
2	Take 3 steps moving sideward L toward center; R stepping behind L, (ct. 1) L to L side

(ct. *and*) R stepping beside L in place (ct. 2). An easier version would be to do the three steps in place.

3-4	Repeat meas. 1-2 above with opp. ftwk. moving away from the center, sideward R, kicking L.
5-8	Repeat kick pattern 2 more times (to make a total of 4 patterns; in, out, in, out).

B. Two-steps, traveling forward, CCW

1	Starting with R, take a forward two-step in LOD; step fwd R, (ct. 1); close L to R and step on it (ct. *and*) step fwd. R (ct. 2)
2-8	Repeat two-step meas. 1 above with opp. ftwk., continue forward around the circle with six more two-steps, alternating lead ft. Total-8 two-steps.

Note: The two-steps may be done in zig-zag patterns; stepping out diag. R with R, stepping behind R with L, stepping diag. R with R; traveling diag. L on next two-step, and so on. An optional variation, once the basic pattern has been mastered, done at the will of the group in a particular line, is to make a CCW turn using 8 two-steps to complete the revolution, wheeling the line in and around to fall in behind the line or lines which have passed by. LH person acts as pivot point. Optional stylistic variations on the kicking action include doing it daintily, heel touching the floor as the leg straightens, kicking higher up in the air, or rotating the kicking leg in and out at the hip joint with each kick.

7. Polka Zu Dreien (Germany)

Polka zu Dreien (PO-ka zu DRY-en) Polka for Three, was taught by Michael and Mary Ann Herman as learned from Paul and Gretel Dunsing. It is also found in the Dunsings' book, *Folk Dances of Germany*. The instructions are adapted from *Folk Dance Syllabus Number One* by Michael Herman, 1953, p. 46.

Music: Folk Dancer MH 1051.

Formation: Sets of three, one man and two women, or vice versa, in a circle of trios in wheelspoke formation, facing CCW (or is sometimes done in a column of 3's) When necessary, this dance can be done with 4 or 5 in a line. Hands joined "W" position with others in line.

Step: Heel-toe polka, plain polka.

Meter 2/4   Dance Pattern

Measures

A. Chorus: Heel-toe Polka in lines

1	Place right heel fwd. on floor (ct. 1); then place R toe in front of left ft, (ct. 2).

2	Take one two-step (or polka step) fwd; step R (ct. 1); close L to R, taking wt. (ct. *and*); step R fwd. (ct. 2)
3-4	Repeat meas. 1 and 2 above with opp. ftwk.
5-8	Repeat meas. 1-4 (total: 4 heel-toe polkas). On last polka or two-step in meas. 8, drop hands and turn individually to face opp. direction (CW), re-joining hands.
9-16	Repeat 4 heel-toe polka steps (meas. 1-8), in opp. direction.

B. Stars with polka step

1-8	Form a RH star with a wrist hold and polka fwd. CW 8 steps.
1-16	Form a LH star, dropping R hands and turning inward to face CCW, polka fwd. CCW 8 polka steps.
1-16	Repeat *Chorus*

C. Circles with polka step

1-8	Join hands and circle left with 8 polka steps (CW).
9-16	Circle right (CCW) with 8 polka steps.

Repeat dance from the beginning until the end of the music.

Dance description included by permission of Michael Herman

8. The Dashing White Sergeant (Scotland)

Music: RCA MH EPA 4128 *Folk Dances for People Who Love Folk Dancing*, ACL 7706 A Jim Cameron Dance Date No. 1 (Ace of Clubs, London).

Formation: Triple Progressive Circle formation; in lines of three (one man between two ladies or vice versa), wheelspoke formation, no. 1 group facing no. 2, no. 3 group facing no. 4, and so on, nos. 1 and 3 CCW, nos. 2 and 4, CW. Center person holds hands of R and LH partners, joined hands held comfortably at shoulder height. Free arms are down at sides or ladies may hold skirts.

Step: Slip step or side slide, skip change of step, setting step (Pas de Basque).

Meter 2/4   Dance Pattern

Measures

1-4	Two facing lines join hands "W" hold in a circle and take 8 (or 7 1/2 plus a hop) sliding steps to left (CW).
5-8	Take 8 sliding steps to R (CCW) in the circle, returning to beginning position in straight lines.
9-10	The center man faces and sets to his ptr. on the R with two Pas de Basque steps, one to the R and one to the L. His RH ptr. does identical pattern.

11-12   Center man turns his RH ptr. with two skip change of steps or two Pas de Basques, joining both hands with her.

13-14   Then he sets to his ptr. on the L and she to him.

15-16   He turns her holding both hands, ending turn by facing his RH ptr. again (2 skip change of steps or Pas de Basques).

17-24   Reels of Three; the three no. 1's in their own line, the three no. 2's in their own line take 8 skip change of steps to trace the same figure 8 from their individual starting points. The center man starts the reel of three by circling CCW his RH ptr., passing *L* shoulders. The LH lady waits until RH lady has come around to face her before starting the figure 8 by passing *R* shoulders with her. Each ends in his or her original place after completing the figure 8.

25-28   The center man takes hands of R and LH ptrs, hands held at shoulder height, and all advance as a line of three toward the opposite line with two skip change of steps and retire with two skip change of steps (forward and back).

29-32   Dropping hands, the three advance toward the opposite line and pass through them, passing R shoulders, to meet the group of three coming toward them, traveling with four skip change of steps.

Dance is repeated with each successive line of three until the end of the music.

Notes adapted from **101 Scottish Country Dances** *by Jean C. Milligan (Collins: Glasgow and London)*

9. Norwegian Mountain March (Denmark-Norway)

Norwegian Mountain March represents two mountain climbers climbing a mountain (presumably Norwegian), with their guide. No. 1 (center person) is the guide and should appear to be pulling the others after him, keeping ahead of them and glancing back to check on their progress. The challenge of the dance lies in untangling the knot smoothly and slowly (as if it were difficult) keeping all handholds unbroken.

Music: LP: *Folk Dances for All Ages*, RCA LPM 1622, Folkraft 1177. Depending on the record, the structure may be ABAB or AABBAABB.

Formation: Groups of three in a triangle formation, preferably, but not necessarily, one man and two women. The middle dancer stands in front (dancer no. 1). Dancer no. 2 stands behind him to his left, dancer no. 3 stands behind him to his right and beside dancer no. 2. All hands are joined, man no. 1 holds woman no. 2's LH in his L, woman no. 3's RH in his R, women no. 2 and 3 join their inside hands. To facilitate the twisting actions, handkerchiefs may be held between joined hands. If no handkerchiefs are used, the

handholds must be loose and flexible. All trios are arranged in a large circle, all facing CCW. Hands remain joined throughout the dance.

Step: Running waltz step (Danish version) or 3/4 slow skip or uneven step-hop (Norwegian version).

Meter 3/4   Dance Pattern

Measures

A. Trios travel fwd CCW with waltz steps (8 meas.)

1-8   Starting R, trios travel fwd. around the circle with 8 running waltz steps, accenting the first beat of each meas. with a stamp. The running waltz steps should be light running steps, three to a measure. As the group travels fwd. (up the mountain), the first dancer (the guide) looks first over his right shoulder at his RH ptr., then over his left shoulder at his LH ptr. checking on his climbers' progress.

B. Intertwining figure-done in place (8 meas.)

9-10   R and LH ptrs. form an arch with their joined inside hands and center person no. 1 backs under the arch with 2 waltz steps (or step-hops), stamping on the first step.

11-12   LH partner, no. 2, moving across in front of no. 1, turns half CW and backs into the space between the center and RH person (no. 3) using two waltz steps. Joined hands must be raised.

13-14   RH ptr. (no. 3) turns left about (CCW) under her own left arm which is joined to LH person (Two waltz steps). Keep all arms raised.

15-16   Center person (no. 1) with two waltz steps, turns R about under his own R arm to end facing forward, his two ptrs. behind him in the original starting position.

Note: If, during the untangling process, the group has swung around to face in a different direction, the leader has plenty of time to re-orient his group toward the original direction.

Repeat entire dance until the end of the music.

E. Level III Dances

1. Free-Style Couple Schottische (International)

Music: Any schottische music, or any music which has an even 4/4 or 2/4 beat and is phrased in 4 meas. of 4/4 or 8 meas. of 2/4. *Walter's Schottische,* Folk Dancer MH-2002-B, Folkraft 1164 or 1166 (45 rpm).

Formation: Couples facing in LOD and traveling in LOD in open or couple position, standing side by side, inside hands joined, or in conversation position, man's R arm around girl's waist, girl's L hand on M's R shoulder. M has his ptr. on his R side. *W does opposite ftwk..*

Step: Walk or run, hop.

Meter 4/4 Dance Pattern

Measures

Basic Pattern

1 Step, close, step, hop (M-L,R,L, hop L) traveling LOD fwd.

2 Step, close, step, hop (M-R,L,R, hop R) traveling LOD fwd.

3 Step L, hop L, step R, hop R, traveling LOD fwd.

4 Step L, hop L, step R, hop R, traveling LOD fwd.

A. Variations to be done during meas. 3 and 4 (step-hops)

Turn as a cpl. CW in shoulder-waist position with 4 step-hops, traveling fwd. LOD at same time, making 2 revolutions.

On 4 step hops, M makes a CCW circle turning to his L and back, while W makes a CW circle turning to her R and back, rejoining hands to begin pattern again moving fwd side by side.

On 4 step-hops, M and W join both hands, face each other and "wring the dishrag," M and W making one complete turn M CCW, W CW, keeping both hands joined and turning under them.

As M continues straight fwd with 4 step-hops, W turns under M's R arm, turning CW one or two turns while step-hopping.

B. Variations to be done during meas. 1 and 2 (Schottische steps)

On first two 1, 2, 3, hops M and W describe a diamond pattern, M moving diag. L and diag. R, W moving diag. R then diag. L, then join hands again to move fwd. on step-hops, or to turn as a cpl.

On ct. 1 of first 1, 2, 3, hop pattern M kneels, and brings W around in front and behind him as she circles him CCW with two 1, 2, 3 hop patterns, his R hand holding her L. M must rise quickly at the end of meas. 2 so that both can step-hop fwd, side by side.

Note: These are only a few of many possible variations to be done in any order or to be interspersed with the basic pattern as the man wishes. The step-close-step-hop is a

Germanic styling. The schottische step can also be done in more open Scandinavian styling as run-run-run-hop.

2. Doudlebska Polka (Czechoslovakia)

Doudlebska polka (DOH-dleb-ska) is a simple mixer learned in Czechoslovakia by Jeannette Novak and introduced to American folk dancers through Folk Dance House, New York.

Music: Folk Dancer MH 3016, Educational Dance Recordings FD-2; Folkraft 1413, LP30..

Formation: Couples in closed position form one large circle or several smaller circles. Directions are for one large circle..

Step: Polka, walk.

Meter 2/4 Dance Pattern

Measures

Note: The directions are for man, lady's part reverse.

1-4 Introduction: no action.

A. Polka

1-16 Beginning left, take 16 polka steps turning CW, traveling in line of direction.

B. Walk and Circle

17-32 Open position, lady's free hand on hip. Man stretches left arm out to place hand on left shoulder of man in front as couples take 32 walking steps moving in line of direction. This action moves dancers toward center to form a ring of couples. As ring revolves counterclockwise, everyone sings "tra-la-la," et cetera.

C. Men Clap, Ladies Circle

33-48 Men face center of circle and clap hands throughout figure as follows: clap own hands (ct. 1), clap own hands (ct. *and*), clap hands of man on both sides, shoulder high (ct. 2). Ladies with hands on hips, take one half-turn CW to face reverse line of direction and take 16 polka steps, progressing forward in reverse line of direction around men's circle.

On last measure, each lady steps behind a man, and men turn around and begin dance again with new partner.

Variations

1-16 For beginners a heavy two-step and the varsouvienne position or inside hands joined may be substituted.

33-48 The men may slap a thigh occasionally, duck down, or cross their own hands over when

Measures	
17-32	they clap neighbors' hands. If group is large , form several small circles.
33-48	If more than one circle is formed, ladies may "cheat" by moving from one circle to another.

Notes: i Those without partners go to the center (the "lost and found" department) and meet the other one without a partner.

ii If there are extra people, extra men without a partner may join dance during star figure, and extra ladies may join ring as ladies polka around outside.

iii Encourage group s*inging* during the march, especially loud. It makes the dance fun!

Dance arranged from the dance description by Michael Herman and reproduced by permission of Folk Dance House, New York, New York.

Above dance description is reproduced as presented in the Fifth Edition (1978) of **Dance A While,** *p. 239, by permission of Jane Harris, Anne Pittman and Marlys Waller.*

3. Bitte Mand I Knibe (Little Man in a Fix) (Denmark)

A very popular little dance, both in Denmark and all over the United States. Knibe means to be in a "spot" or "fix."

Music: Record: Aqua Viking V400; Folk   Dancer MH 1054; Tanz 58401, EZ 6009.
Piano: Burchenal, E., *Folk Dances of Denmark,* p. 44, and *Folk Dances from Old Homelands,* p. 62.

La Salle, D., *Rhythms and Dances for Elementary Schools,* p 115.

Formation: Two couples, lady to right of partner. Men hook left elbows and place right arm around partner's waist, ladies place left hand on man's left shoulder..

Step: Running step, tyrolian waltz, waltz.

Meter 3/4	Dance Pattern

Measures

Note: Directions are same for man and lady, except when specially noted.

A. Run Around

1-8	Beginning left, take small running steps forward, moving CCW. Couples lean away from pivot point.
1-8	As *running steps are continued,* men grasp left hands and raise left arms, holding ladies' left hand with their right and two ladies move under arch and pass each other. Ladies turn

CCW to face center, men lower left arms and ladies grasp each other's right hand on top of men's left-hand grasp. All four continue to take small running steps, moving CCW.

B. Tyrolian Waltz

9-12	Men release left hand, ladies right. The two couples turn back to back. Each couple takes couple position, inside hands shoulder height, outside arm relaxed at side. Man beginning left, lady right, take four tyrolian waltz steps moving in line of direction. Arms reach forward and draw back with each step. They do not swing forward.
13-16	Closed position. Man beginning left, lady right, take four waltz steps, turning CW, progressing in line of direction.
9-16	Repeat action of meas. 9-16.

Note: As the dance repeats, each couple dances with another couple. If a couple cannot find a couple for the first figure, they are *in a fix*! They go to the center and dance the running steps alone, with two hands joined. The next time the man will avoid being the *man in a fix* by hooking arms with another couple quickly for the first figure.

Above dance description is reproduced as presented in the Fifth Edition (1978) of **Dance A While** *p. 230 by permission of Jane Harris, Anne Pittman and Marlys Waller.*

Appendix I
Annotated List of Selected Resource References

1. Books
Key:

A. Information on teaching techniques and progressions, step analysis, evaluation, class projects, etc.

B. Ethnic background information

C. Dance Descriptions
Note: There are many books of dance descriptions available. The ones listed below are some for which records are likely to be currently obtainable in the United States or Canada.

D. Costume information and construction
Note: For pictures of authentic costumes, the National Geographic magazines are an invaluable source. Also, local ethnic groups often have costumes brought from their homelands which may be copied. The books listed below give ideas for easily-made approximations.

Berk, Fred. *Ha-Rikud The Jewish Dance,* American Zionist Youth Foundation, Union of American Hebrew Congregations, 1972. *B,C.*

Czarnowski, Lucile K. *Folk Dance Teaching Cues,* The National Press, Palo Alto, Calif., 3rd. ed., 1963. *A, C.*

Duggan, Anne S., Schlottmann, Jeanette, Rutledge, Abbie. *The Teaching of Folk Dance,* The Ronald Press Co., New York, 1948. *A, B.*

Folk Dance Federation of California, Inc. *Costumes Simple to Make,* 1275 "A" Street, Hayward, California 94541, 1970. *D.*

---------------. *Costume Basics,* 1975. *D.*

---------------. *Dances from Near and Far* Series: 6 Volumes - A-1, A-2, Beginning, B-1, B-2, Intermediate, C-1 Advanced, D-1 Dances Without Partners. *C.*

Gault, Marian and Ned. *100 and 1 Easy Folk Dances,* 1970. *C.* and *100 and 1 More Easy Folk Dances,* 1977. *C.*
(obtainable from Festival Folk Shop)

Gilbert, Cecile. *International Folk Dance at a Glance,* Burgess Publishing Co., 1974. *A, C.*

Harris, Jane A., Pittman, Anne, and Waller, Marlys. *Dance A While,* Burgess Publishing Company, Minneapolis, Minnesota, Fifth Edition, 1978. *A, B, C, D.*

Holden, Rickey, and Vouras, Mary. *Greek Folk Dances,* Folkraft Press, Newark, New Jersey, 1965. *B, C.*

Jensen, Mary Bee and Jensen, Clayne R. *Folk Dancing,* Brigham Young University Press, Provo, Utah, 1974. *A, C, D.*

Joukowsky, Anatol. *The Teaching of Ethnic Dance,* J. Lowell Pratt and Co., New York, 1965. *B, C.*

Lidster, Miriam D. & Tamburini, Dorothy. *Folk Dance Progressions,* Wadsworth Publishing Co., 1965. *A, B, C.*

Lidster, Miriam D. *Teaching Progressions for Folk Dancers,* Miriam Lidster, Stanford University, 1975. *A, C.*

Milligan, Jean C. *101 Scottish Country Dances,* Collins, Glasgow and London, 1956. *A, B, C.*

Mynatt, Constance V. and Kaiman, Bernard K. *Folk Dancing for Students and Teachers,* Wm. C. Brown Co., Publishers, Dubuque, Iowa, 1968. *A, C.*

Petrides, Theodore and Elfleida. *Folk Dances of the Greeks,* Exposition Press, New York, 1961. *B, C.*

2. Record Shops

Canadian Folk Dance Service
Can.-Ed. Media Ltd.
185 Spadina Ave., Ste. 1
Toronto, Ontario M5T 2C6

Festival Folk Shop
2769 W. Pico
Los Angeles, Calif. U.S.A. 90006

Folk Music International
Worldtone Music Inc.
230 7th Ave.
New York, New York U.S.A. 10011

Glamar Dancecraft Limited
3584 East Hastings
Vancouver, B.C.
291-2026

Appendix II
Folk Dance Organizations

Canadian Folk Arts Council/
Le Conseil Canadien des Arts Populaires
1499 De Bleury, Ste. 200,
Montreal, Quebec H3A 2H5
Contact: Yves Moreau

Canadian Folk Society, Vancouver Branch
(information about ethnic groups)
contact: Frances Fridge (Mrs. T. G. Fridge)
5560 Columbia, Vancouver, B.C.
327-3316

Folk Dance Federation of California, North
Contact: Carol Scholin
931 Flint Ave.
Concord, California, U.S.A.
94518

Folk Dance Federation of California, South
13250 Ida Ave.
Los Angeles, California, U.S.A. 90066
213-398-9398

Northwest Folkdancers, Inc. (Information about clubs, festivals, workshops in B.C., Montana, Washington, Oregon)
President (1980): Nelle Goldade
3409 - 172nd S. W.
Lynnwood, Washington, U.S.A. 98036

Ontario Folk Dance Association
President (1980): Diane Gladstone
483 Rushton Rd.
Toronto, Ontario M6 C 2Y4